# qarrtsiluni
online literary magazine

I0549093

*Qarrtsiluni is an experiment in online literary and artistic collaboration. The title comes from an Iñupiaq word that means "sitting together in the darkness, waiting for something to burst."*

*The online journal began publishing on September 20, 2005; our first print issue was the September-December issue, 2008.*

*We encourage you to visit our website, where in addition to all the material presented here, you will find audio files of the authors reading their own work, music and video contributions to the theme, full-color reproductions of all the images, comments from readers, and responses from the authors.*

www.qarrtsiluni.com

*Beth Adams and Dave Bonta*

managing editors

*Brittany Larkin*

editorial assistant

ISBN 978-0-9866909-0-7

PHOENICIA PUBLISHING
MONTREAL

# words of power

september-december 2009

Come words of power, we said, and fill our inboxes. Come curses and spells, charms and prayers, come incantations, imprecations, castigations, come. Let mantras and holy scripture ladder us down where the bright ore of symbolic language first glittered in the light of a caveman's torch. Let oaths bleed into legal instruments; let the party of the first part depart. Who has ears to hear, listen the fuck up.

Let words precise as snow crystals give birth to a wild meltwater roar: blessings, namings, signs and rules, writs and contracts. Come words of angry widows, cheating wives, absent fathers, forgotten sons; words to bind us and release us, words that label and ensnare. Come, longed-for words and those remembered, words that enlarged us, diminished, words thundering into life or struggling out of silence.

Let tongues burn with the fire of prophets and bellies knot with the solemn pronouncements of law.

Come, words of power: be recited — or go unsaid.

Let the cloroform of text still your shivery wings.

*Dave Bonta and Beth Adams*
editors

# Contents

# words of power

*Dedicated to the memory of Harvey Parker*

# Lung Ta (wind words)

*Dorothee Lang*

"It's simple," he explained. "You put up the flags in a high place — and the wind carries their mantras into all pervading spaces that are in need of them."

# Ceremony: the Opening of the Mouth

*Alex Cigale*

May my heart be with me in the house of hearts
May it be given back to me among the living
May it toll and mete out a steady measure

Though daily I am seen rolling my past
like a ball of dung in front of my face
with pincer-like paws — the resurrection —

I am born anew in the rising sun
singing the random code of combinations
keys to the kingdom of everlasting life

Arise ye to the boats you wise boatmen
to the recitation of parts — masts sails oars
rudders — mechanisms of struggle for control

Commit to memory the many names
and the many gates of the doorkeepers
internal strictures and structures of soul

Great power resides in appellations
under ancient laws a slave had no name
and thus no function as a legal person

Forbidden to label compelled to invent —
physical body the shadow the full title —
panoply of names that death may not find me

# Go My Uncle and Fetch the Bride

*Jane Rice*

1.

Under the road
a floor

black heat kidnaps the sun

and the desert planes land, land, land

soldiers float dreams
in shallow-
dug holes

as if they need
only width of shoulders
length: with boots

as if they scoop
fading light
to keep it

world of stories below
spring from the sea

2.

Who remembers
the tree
the garden

words make faces
something
lies in wait

side street
of trembling

labyrinth
arms itself
with branches

stream trickles
no wider
than a wrist

who
remembers
pebbles

hand's gray face
nostrils on fire
shaken

eyes echo

each voice
of a candle
sings to the tree

3.

Little thing
like distance

soldiering a nest
of stones

smoke fans gray
and gray
fans smoke

fluke of breath
revives

sky of crushed
tilts wandering

the word earth
limited to land

amounts
to flight

charcoal tree
against the mountain

as are pronouns for those
not in the room

one plus one equals *and*
distinct
not interchangeable

ears weep
even if eyes
refuse

dust of nameless inks
remember the tree all green

\*

Note: A 16th century poem, know as L'Chah Dodi, is sung at Friday night services to welcome the sabbath bride. There are many variations on the tune and numerous translations. The literal translation of the first line is *Go my uncle towards bride*. I heard it translated as *Go my uncle and fetch the bride*. I loved that translation much better than another version I had read: *Beloved, come to meet the bride* (or) *Let's go, my friend, towards the bride*. This summer I was studying prayer-book Hebrew as part of my process of converting to Judaism. We were studying possessives, hence an explanation of "my" uncle.

# St Joseph of Cupertino. 9/18

*Wendy Vardaman*

Maybe it's the lighthead — wanting
in mental capacity so that when Joseph studies
for a test, he focuses on one item only. Prays
for his examiners to ask that question. Flying,
however, comes easily, happens trancing
on God, involuntary; one minute he's
with his fellow Franciscans, the next he's taken off. It happens
first on the order's feast day, then with increasing

frequency. He can't stop, poor empty-
handed priest, no matter the ascending rank of those who order
him not to make a spectacle of himself.
Exiled by the pope to Assisi then to one commune and the next, he goes dry,
ordered not to speak to anyone other
than his bishop, until the last mass, Assumption Day, overcome by happiness, he lifts off.

# Cuss Club

*Ian Singleton*

Randy and his mom always moved to new places. This was the third place since I became friends with Randy. It was a townhouse where we could sneak out onto the granular slant of the roof and see the lights of Chattanooga. The gush of water from the spout, the clang of pots and pans in the sink, and light from the kitchen would signal if his mom was coming and we needed to dodge back into his bedroom. He held up his hand when the kitchen noise hushed and the light flipped off.

You wanna stay over next Friday? We can go out in the woods and cuss.

Next Friday was such a long time from that Sunday, so I just said yeah. He shushed me when we heard the door to his room open.

Randy, his mom recited. Then the door shut.

I been learning from my cousins from Nashville. They taught me, he splayed his fingers, five new ones. We can go say em in the woods.

I was through the window as soon as he rose. Just as his foot touched the carpeting, the door swung open and his mom asked, Where you been Randy?

We was hiding under the bed, ma. Tricked you.

Randy, I was looking for you. Gil's gotta go home now. Gil, did you call your parents?

No, ma'am.

Well, I think you need to call them.

Yes, ma'am.

\*\*\*

Both my parents came to pick me up.

Did you have fun?

I shrugged my shoulders.

I hope you had fun. Miss Byson just keeps moving further and further away from us. We had to cut through the city from the theater. It's quicker, but you have to go through some bad parts of town.

What Randy said came from my mouth as, Hey mom can I please stay the night with Randy next Friday?

They both stayed silent while we passed houses with wooden windows and people huddled around a loud car. We sped up and cuffed a bump in the road. I could see a long line of street lights, all the color of pee.

Gilly, I just said—

Mom, don't call me Gilly.

Say please. Show some manners when you talk to your mother, said my dad.

Gil, she continued, I just finished telling you it's a long drive for you to come out to see Randy. Why can't he come out to our house?

I don't know, I said.

Maybe his mom is tired after work. Maybe she can't afford the gas, my dad answered.

My mom gripped his arm. Gilly—I mean, Gil? You wanna ask him over to our house?

But we don't have woods.

Yes we do. We have the woods out by the golf course. What used to be Shiners' Gully.

I don't know if they'll be safe in there, Burt.

Well, said my dad, Lord knows where they're going when they're out here. It's just a bunch of apartment complexes, he mumbled.

Okay I get it, my mom said. How come you wanna go to Randy's on Friday and you already decided to ask, my mom said glancing at me.

My dad's deep voice echoed. I said, I'm gonna show him Shiners' Gully. Can I ask Brandon and Terry?

My mom only shook her head and my dad, turning onto the right fork of the road, said, Well we're out of it.

\*\*\*

I stood far away from Randy. My mom would have taken us to Papa Joe's pizza and the arcade but he wanted to go in the woods. His mom never took us out. Brandon hissed and shook his head. Terry watched Brandon and I kicked the bottom step.

My mom smiled and climbed back up the stairs. I heard her walking around up there through the ceiling.

Y'all wanna go out there? Y'all ready?

Ready for what, said Brandon.

You'll see, said Randy tucking his feet into his slipons.

Brandon snickered and we filed out the front door and across the street. The woods were not far and after cutting through a short stretch of trees we dropped down the slope. Shiners' Gully was only fifteen minutes across. But it was steep. Jagged logs had washed up along the banks and nested against one another.

Brandon was the first to cuss. Shit, he said when he slipped and landed on his butt in the mud. Randy just stared at him with a solid gaze, his eyes like black-eyed peas. I waited for him to cuss. He only twitched his nose like he was excited by a smell, then bounded to the gully bed.

The ground was sludge and gave off a swamp stench. My last two steps had caused my feet to sink under past the ankle. I just stood stuck there until I heard Randy laughing. You look like you wanna cuss, he said.

Man I'm not going down there, said Brandon.

C'mon now, said Randy. Let's cuss.

That looks nasty down there, said Terry.

You wanna know one, asked Randy. He flung his arms and rocked on his heels, squishing the mud I had fallen in.

What, said Brandon.

You wanna learn some cuss words, asked Randy.

Cusses, said Brandon. That's why you brought us out here?

Randy's eyes narrowed and his mouth stayed open, like it was ready for anything to come out. I thought I could see his freckles vibrating. Shit, he said. Then he said, Fucker.

You just brought us out here so you could cuss? Why didn't you just cuss at home?

Randy still smiled but his voice was softer and his breath was heavy. Cause a mom might hear us, he half-asked half-said.

Are you retarded, asked Terry.

Shit. Fuck, said Randy. C'mon! I know shit, fuck, ass, cunt, and bastard.

Do you know what any of those mean?

Randy chewed a couple times and said, My cousins taught em to me.

I know what all of them mean, said Brandon.

So, said Randy.

So, you're stupid. I know what they mean—you don't.

So, said Randy. I was gonna teach em to Gil. Gil don't know em.

Brandon's icy eyes fixed on me and he set his hands on his hips. Terry pinched his nose and shook his head. You don't know curses, Gil?

Fuck, I said. Shit, I said. Fuck you, I said aimed at Randy. Ass, I said. Fuck you cunt, I said. Then, You bastard. Fuck you, bastard.

Bet he knows what that one means, said Terry behind Brandon as if he was whispering.

Randy's fists balled. His jaw grinded. His eyes pooled.

\*\*\*

I only saw Randy once more after that day. I was hurrying along the tile floor of the mall searching for Brandon and Terry who had played a game where they yelped and covered their noses and mouths like I stunk that bad, then ran away and hid. I had to find them.

A growl from behind made me flip around. It was Randy. He was glaring at me with a grin across his face. His upper lip was curling, baring his teeth. He still hadn't learned to curse.

Fuck. You're a fuck. You're a fucking shitty dick. You're a fucking bitch. Bitch.

Once he started using new words, I turned around and kept walking. He cursed louder and followed. I noticed people wincing, eyeing him from the stores. Fucker. Fuck you. Shit.

There was one word he would never use. I kept searching for my friends. I rounded corners and stepped out onto the bridge to the parking deck. He broke off at the glass doors and watched me, glaring at me while I tried to ignore him. Finally, I forgot he was there.

# "Om Sai Ram" A Thousand Times

*Patricia Bralley*

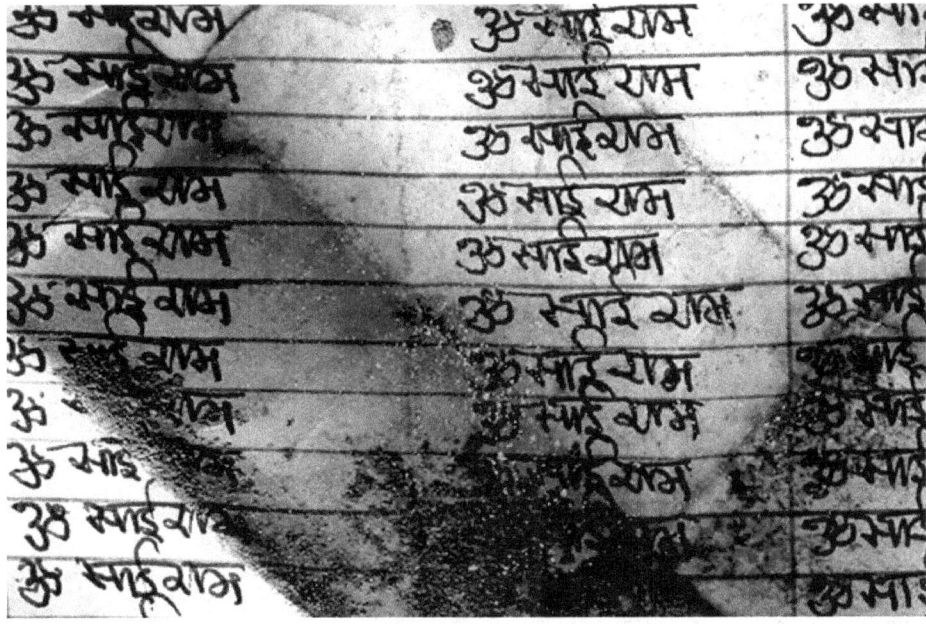

Over twenty years ago my mother brought from India samples of the sacred ash, *vibhuti*.

Ash is all that remains after wood is burnt away. And in a similar manner, God as imperishable Truth is that which remains when all names and forms are dissolved.

Sathya Sai Baba, considered by many to be an incarnation of the divine, is fond of materializing *vibhuti* for his devotees. This ash is carefully wrapped in small paper packets constructed from sheets of paper upon which devotees have inscribed *Om Sai Ram* — a thousand times, ten thousand times — in their longing to find God.

This image is of one such packet that has been in my dresser drawer all these years.

While not a follower of Baba, I do regard the *vibhuti* as something of a modern day miracle not unlike blood appearing on the crucifix or tears from a Madonna.

*Editors' Note: "Om" is a universal mantra. "Sai," a name for God, can be divided into "Sa" (universal father) and "Ai" (universal mother); the guru is also considered to be both mother and father to the devotees. "Ram" is an abbreviated form of "Rama", often translated simply as "God" in English. "Ra" is the Fire Principle, which burns all to ash, while "ma" stands for maya or illusion, so together, they mean the destruction of illusion.*

*Patricia adds, "Perhaps ultimately it's not about words. With sacred language the heart transcends the surface meaning and delivers the celestial."*

# Dear Brain

*Muriel Karr*

*(lavish love letter, written in the hope of ending*
*severe migraines; the ruse didn't work)*

Beloved brain, precious seat-of-emotion amygdala,
how hard you have worked to make me who I am. O pons,
much-praised cerebellum; fourth ventricle, observed
in my atlas of human anatomy; nuclei and fiber bundles,
long may ye wave, though I may not have mentioned you before.

I live in gratitude, despite any moaning, for your complexities,
dear brain. Your pathways, your receptors; how you integrate
motor signals. Medulla oblongata, hippocampus, colliculi;
occipital lobe, gray and white matter, mammillary bodies:
have I told you lately how much I love you?

I love to speak your name, though I consider you
not Broca's, but mine, dear brain. O cranial nerves,
did my switch of handedness from left to right
disturb you? Does all flow as it should, in your cerebral
aqueduct? I want, even cherish, your over-excitable cells.

Tell me what food I should feed you: I will provide.
You will be massaged; caressed. Iced, if needed, when vessels
expand with blood; I will shrink what ails you; comfort
with cool hands. You afford me, dear brain, a peerless mind
connecting dots as no other. Let me count the ways.

# Maledictus Requiescat

*Juleigh Howard Hobson*

Oh may your casket smother you because
You won't be buried dead. And may you wake
In ground-chill dark, 6 feet below, mistake
Your ability to free yourself, sores
Sprouting from your fingertips as you try
To pry, to claw, to push your panicked way
Out of your prescribed resting place. I pray
And will that you won't drop dead too fast. I
Will that you suffer. I will your breath to
Come in hard-laboured oxygen-starved waves:
Short and incomplete. I want all the graves
Around to shudder as you suck the few
Final molecules of breathable air
Into your lungs, alone, alone, down there.

# The Word

*Susan Roney-O'Brien*

He liked his girl
innocent, and when on her knees at twelve
she refused to pray, said
she was too tired, didn't believe anyway,
then told him what the boy across the street had whispered,
that *fuck* that lit up his mouth
what his squat fingers had done
clamping the front of her shirt like a crab,
her father backed her into a closet,
unbuckled his belt and slammed it
hard across her bare ass
but it took so long for her to scream
that when she did that word escaped
fueled his arm, and her mother ran
upstairs to stop him but
stopped herself instead when she saw his face
and remembered the taste of his belt on her flesh,
watched the strap land again and again
until blood fell and he stepped back
turned from his wife in tears, the girl
gasping the same bad word until
cool cloths and dreams did their work.
Apologies became denials and
grew into a forest of thorns
nobody could see
and the girl didn't know if
what she remembered was real
or a bad dream because she had swallowed
the thorns and they flowered
inside like a secret she never told
even when she married, and one night
when her husband, backing her down to
keep her in line with a few gut punches
where the bruises wouldn't show
unclamped the brass buckle from his jeans
and jerked the leather belt from beneath his belly
to teach her to keep her goddamned mouth
shut, to get her to screw when he
wanted her to, that closet door
unhinged like a jaw and thorns made stone,

honed to diamond points, gleamed through,
and she ran to the kitchen, grabbed
the butcher knife from its slit in the block
and caught him, slashed the soft pink swell
of his gut, screaming
*fuck fuck fuck* in her head
but making no sound at all.

# The Rules

*Christopher Woods*

# Kol Nidre

*Peg Duthie*

At last year's service, she wore espadrilles
fashioned from a jacket she used to wear
to other people's weddings. So many vows
polluted with the ashes of bridges. If
she believed in God, she'd have to berate Him
even more than she already does each time
she scrapes the sludge of sloughed-off oaths
from her well-tanned soul, or when she trims
cookie-cutter blasphemies out of her mind's
ruthless replaying of her sins. *Sloppy work,*
she tells Him. *I can't love anyone*
*proud of setting me up to fail.* Yet, the years
she pretended the holidays weren't hers,
she felt like an incomplete book, like a spine
losing its glue, pages dropping away
before their time. So now, each fall,
she brings home apples and honey, and wears
fabric shoes to shul the following week, chanting
a counterpoint within her mind
at every iteration of the Kaddish.

# Naming the Flowers

*Ron Czerwien*

Mother's Affliction
Inflamed Iris
Lady Sliver
Cemetery Skin
Prickly Bitch
Wad-of-Red-Cellophane
Queen Anne's Head
Dab-of-pus
Fuckin-thorn
Deadly Lampshade
Bachelor's Buttocks
Vining-Back-Hair
Whimpering Pansy
Face-down-in-the-muck
Lone Gunman
Flowering Chest Wound
Hateful Neighbor
Jack-in-the-forehead
House-in-flames
Swan Parts
Angel's "Trumpet"
Touch-me-here
Bloody Ha Ha
Silver Phlegm
Purple Discharge
Sweet Tumor
Wild Corpse
Annual Contagion
Baby's Claw
Dainty Hemorrhage
Everlasting-facial-tick
Surgical Mishap
Stitched Eye Sack
Mucus Cups
Tainted Tongue
Creepy Jennie
Broom-rape
Black-eyed Mistress
Yew Prick
Joe Pie

# Lust in Translation

*Bryan Borland*

Between gulps of syllables
you said you wanted to speak my language,
the coded initiation to our lesson
that would leave nouns and adjectives
covering my body in your slanted handwriting,
the roughness of your voice,
the words "cocksucker" and "faggot"
lost in translation, my burning ears
heard "baby" and "please."
With your penis in my mouth
it always seemed I held the power
of vocabulary.
You slapped my face,
I felt a caress.
You pulled my hair like a proud older brother.
"Swallow it bitch" was a love note I kept
for years
folded in my back pocket.

# Brink

*Anne Morrison Smyth*

# The Burrowing Song

*Karen Greenbaum-Maya*

A song burrowed into a woman's head. It got in when someone said, "Oh, that's just dandy." C&H, C&H, Mommy uses it to bake her cakes. She makes the greatest cookies cakes and candy — they're dan-dan-dandy! When the woman was in her bed, she could hear it upstairs.

C&H, C&H, Mommy uses it to bake her cakes. The woman called a pest control service, the one with the man dressed like an undertaker and carrying a big heavy mallet. She asked them to kill the song. It needs to be fed, they said, don't you have some cookies, cakes or candy? "Oh, that's just dandy," the woman told them, and then she wept. Her blood pressure went up, so her GP prescribed meds. The song still played, only now in a chromatic scale, like Bach gone inbred.

Finally, the woman packed up her red Keds and left the house. The song had become part of the plumbing and stayed behind. Cool, she thought, at last I've got the damned thing balked. Who is the coolest guy who is what am? Fast-talking slow-walking good-looking Mohair Sam.

Now she has a safe tune and always carries it with her. If she sings it silently, the safe tune can drive away a burrowing song.

# Prayers

*David Need*

*From "St John's Rose Slumber," XVII*

This porch among fallen winters
space of my hand
on your shoulder

\*\*\*\*

a secret room behind the books
your daughter's footsteps
on stairs to the basement

\*\*\*\*

body becomes field
and so can answer sun, "asters"
and so wait

\*\*\*\*

fire
no longer secret
is autumn
my father's diagram

\*\*\*\*

a priest lazy in a field
careless
mistakes ideas
for flowers

\*\*\*\*

oh, rose
split
makes possible
the hidden skies

\*\*\*\*

face, first of all, prow
filled with water
your cupped hands

\*\*\*\*

what moves in them
but fallen winters
your shoulder ahead

\*\*\*\*

a translation to kiss
as I am shadows
her daughter

\*\*\*\*

and so founded

\*\*\*\*

so you also
speak stones across the river
spark

\*\*\*\*

a path back
inside myself
lifts dream

\*\*\*\*

skirt lifted
her feet descend
a last ridge

****

ocean rose
blueblack in her hair
and iris

****

eyes shut lips shut
ears shut      the shuttered doors
of icons

****

a candle guttered
a city became shepherd
these for you

****

majesty

****

in star folds

****

in your pocket.

# Incantation For My Old Friend, Landers

*Alex Cigale*

Thunder, thunder, lightning, storm,
let the next three days be gone.

Northern cloud front, western sun,
while the southerlies have come.

Wind is rising at my back,
Washington Bridge traffic, trucks.

Willing weather: heal me, heel,
or all else miserable.

It has rained four forty days,
left me stewing in my daze.

Mark my word, the water's line
will keep rising in your mind.

Beer, port, vodka, whiskey, wine,
just 'bout now would be de-vine.

# Incantations Over Alloys

*Kaz Sussman*

*for the carburetor gladiator*

O spirit of alloys, valves and kin
I sacrifice to you my knuckle skin.
O floating butterfly choke and rotor
get the juice to the damn motor.
O spirit of alloys, valves and kin
I sacrifice to you my knuckle skin.
Spark, fire and suck up fuel,
grant me luck and work now tool.
O spirit of alloys, valves and kin
I sacrifice to you my knuckle skin.
Choke it out easy, bleed out the glitch,
work now tool, you son of a bitch!

# The Smiling Beaks of Bluebirds

*Christi Krug*

The packing list said *sunscreen, sleeping bag, trail mix*. I would tame the wild woods with *flashlight* and *wool socks*. But the word *swimming suit* choked my mind with unknown waters.

I'd been living with Grandma since fall, and nobody seemed to know how long it would last. We didn't discuss Mother's illness, only that she was "sick," and "in the hospital." But it was the most frightening hospital I'd ever seen, where a teenage girl with a crewcut sat hollow-eyed in a TV room, and an old lady shuffled back and forth holding a doll, and a bearded man with a greasy T-shirt talked to a plant.

Not to mention Mother, dressed in a bathrobe, moving slow as if she were drowning. Speaking in a flat, faraway voice, with eyes that looked in your direction but didn't see. There was a breadcrumb in the corner of her lips.

Now it was summer. No talk about fall, past or future. "You're going to camp," said Grandma. The only words I had were mysterious, in Helvetica typeface, next to tidy checkboxes.

*Pillow*, I read. Out loud I said, "Camera."

"You can borrow my Instamatic," said Grandma. She frowned and tapped a pen against her lips.

I looked at that one word again. It reminded me that I could not swim. It told me I might drown.

"It's only for a month," Grandma added. "A whole month! You'll have So. Much. Fun."

The last word on the list was *stationery*. Grandma wrote letters every week on her Smith-Corona typewriter. Letters were what you did when you couldn't do anything else. When home couldn't hold the right people, at the right time.

I stood in the parking lot, sun gleaming off the gravel. Grandma gave me a peck on the cheek and handed me a package just as I was about to board the bus. It was a see-through box tied with blue ribbon: stationery topped with bluebirds. Their beaks smiled grandly.

Two hours later, the Hidden Valley Camp bus turned out into wide, green fields bordered by forest.

Two days later, I knew the names of everyone in my tent, and what they got in the mail. Stacy got a care package of chocolate chip cookies. Jenny got a troll doll. Terri got a very small pillow with white daisies. I got a letter from Mother.

The return address was *Western State Psychiatric Hospital*. On the stamped letterhead, Mother's penciled handwriting sagged like a sprung spiderweb. She wrote, *I forget if it's two or three sentences to a paragraph.*

When I was five, I used to lean against the window and cry whenever Mother left. Now I crumpled her letter in my hands.

\*\*\*

"Canoe time," Counselor said, some days after. Stacy and Jenny cheered. Terri said, "All riiight!" I shivered at the water's edge.

I don't know how I made it into the boat, fat in my orange life jacket. Then I dipped my oar in the blue-green lake of shadows and it was easy. Like sticking fingers into frosting and pulling away a smooth, silky hunk. It was like mirror writing, the way you paddled opposite how you wanted to move.

After, I sat on the dock with my tentmates, dabbling toes in the ripples. The warm wood scratched my thighs.

"I saw 'The Omen' before camp," said Stacy. "It's rated 'R' but my Dad takes me to any movie I want. It scared the hell out of me."

"Yeah?" said Jenny.

"In 'The Omen,' there's this kid, Damien. His parents don't know where he comes from. He's a child of Satan."

And with three words, the terror was back. *Child of Satan* told me everything I needed to know. The water wouldn't kill me. Neither would it kill me to have a mother in the mental hospital. But this was the ultimate terror, and the reason I felt different from the other kids: I was a child of Satan.

The truth of it was a shadow, thick and empty, filling my stomach. I fed on it at night in my sleeping bag, the trees whispering about the canvas tent walls. It exhausted me at craft time. *Child of Satan.* It yanked me from the inside and outside, stretching me until I was thin and see-through like the taffy we pulled at Group Activity.

Three weeks, those words threaded through my mind.

Then, one day in the woods, I forgot to think them.

Our hike leader led us high along the forest trail. At last she said, "Okay, guys. Lean your heads back. Look up to the highest branches. Squinch your eyes. Can you see how different everything looks?"

There was a shine that wiggled in the treetops, like soap bubble liquid stretched over a

---

plastic hoop. The light was changing, things were shimmering. Walking back to camp, I saw a *trail mix* of leaves and mushrooms, frosted ponds, sugar-daddy creeks. Old trees offered friendly, knobby hands. The creek was not afraid to sing.

That night, Jenny, Stacy, Terri and I held flashlights to our chins, laughing as our faces glowed molten red, changing from human to alien. I took out my packet of bluebird stationery.

>Dear Mom,
>
>I was very happy to hear from you! I'm going to tell you a little about this camp. There are many different things to do. There is Archery, Rifelery, Hikes, Riding horses, special events, sailing, canoeing, swimming, sports, overnights. Its hard to think of everything... Camp fires. Every person has to do something around the tent. One day you might be the sweeper. Another day you might be the Person that puts up the Tent flaps. Everything is fun. Hope your glad to hear from me! Love ya!!
>
>Love, Christy
>
>P.S. I'm beginning to miss everyone a little.

When camp was over, Grandma met the camp bus, tapping my shoulder with her driving glove, ready to hit the road. A month later, she would put me in a foster home.

For years, Mother would save my letter, shuttling the bluebird pages from drawer to suitcase, from dresser to shoebox, in the halfway houses and care facilities where she spent her life. Home would never again mean having her with me.

I stopped crumpling Mother's letters when they came. I answered them, putting down my thoughts — even when they were bright and flighty and fake as bluebirds that smiled. In this way, I learned to make my own magic words.

# book of spells

*andrew topel*

# The New Dogma

*C. Albert*

Thou shalt not beg,
bite, bark incessantly
nor steal biscuits.

Before the Dog Prophecies
there was only ignorance
and fleas.

Follow the righteous
path to the dog park.

Sit and stay,
Roll over,
Do not eat grass.

Praise ye the one Dog

who smites evil
with thy paws,

who giveth bones
to the hungry—

Hallelujah!

# Learning to Curse

*Ann E. Michael*

Regaining breath, he
undoubles slowly
his back to the schoolyard's
chainlink fence, too
surprised to swear.
His enemies grinned
with the cruel fear
of boys and skimmed
off with his pals
down alleyways
their crowing still
lodged in his gut—
slurs he could not refute
with his fists. Half-crawls
to the spot by the tetherball
pole where they collect
at recess and retches
up his humiliation,
wipes his hot face
with his damp wrist,
heads home with
each breath new
in his raw
throat, muttering
shit shit shit
to the five o'clock
suburban sidewalk.

# Grandmother Praying

*Oriana*

*Veronika, first i.d. photo (1945) after Auschwitz*

## Saint Anthony

Pincushions, hairnets,
a mischievous spool of thread;
thimbles wobble in uneven hoops,
needles enter the veins of things.

We rummage through drawers
reeking of decayed *Soir de Paris*
cologne and valerian drops;
the slipper-hedged dusk under the bed.

There remains the invisible world.
We kneel on the creaking floor
before the painting of a smiling monk,
a lily like a magic wand

tilting from his hand.
With a practiced zigzag,
we cross ourselves: *Saint Anthony,*
*guide us to Grandmother's thimble*
Again we scan
the summits of wardrobes,
horizons of floors;
the precipice behind the couch,

gritty crevasses of chairs.
She gives up at last:
*The devil must have*
*covered it with his tail.*

## God's Hearing

One evening in Auschwitz
the women in her barracks began to pray.

Their prayer grows and grows,
a chant, a moan, a howl —
it carries far into the searchlight-blinded,

electric wire-razored night.
The Kapo rushes in, shouting, *Not*
*so loud! God is not hard of hearing!*

And my grandmother laughs.
Then she starts an old hymn:
*Many have fallen*

*in the sleep of death,*
*but we have still awakened*
*to praise Thee,*

she sings to the God of Auschwitz.
Her voice does not quiver.

# From Genesis Rabbah

*James Toupin*

Across the centuries,
you hear the Catskills cadence —
Thus Rab Ezekiel,
as his son, Rabbi Judah,
recounted: "Why shall we bless
the name of God for giving
us each drop of rain?"
One. Two. Three.
Four. The pause that strums
the crowd. "Because it could
be coming down in sheets."

Of course, rabbinic texts
do not record a rim shot,
and maybe the son forgot
his father's way with a set-up
(sons can have tin ears),
yet like a great joke straddling
the ambiguities
the sage's punch line sits
poised between two stools,
the one a blasphemy,
giving thanks for the absence
of God as Father of Floods,
the other sublime madness,
attempting a prayer
for each drop as it falls.

And of what would the prayer
consist? "Blessed art thou,
O Lord our God, Ruler
of the Universe,
who laughs, just this once, with us."

# Going Out to Buy Shoes

*Richard Nester*

It was around that time that my wife's
father decided to run for office, mayor
of heaven, I think it was. He campaigned
from his chair as I wheeled him around
the mall. It was extraordinary. The shoppers
had never seen such friendliness. He made
everyone smile whether they wanted to or not.
Imagine an antic child, who fathoms
what no child can, our covetousness and cruelty,
because it's his. "Smile," he shouted
to everyone, waving his bony hands,
as we passed the corner of Butterfly
and Butterfly. "You may not get
another chance." Later on, he asked me
for a riding crop so he could switch
the uncompliant ones. It takes a certain
meanness, I admit, to wring love from thieves
and liars. Sure, he knows. But it was love,
not pity, in their eyes he said, and that
was good. "If I'd had an education,
I'd be dangerous," he added, about himself,
work done, chewing a cheese sandwich
with his one tooth.

# Yoga Center Wall

*Steve Wing*

# The Man who Spoke the Law

*James Brush*

*Old folks will tell you there was a time when there was no poetry. Not around here anyway. Maybe back east or some place where time was more available, but breaking this land took all a man had and didn't leave anything for him at the end. Certainly, no time for pretty words.*

*Some will even tell you that there was laws against it, but I don't hold with that story. Still, I had this idea for a poem, back in '08 or so and I didn't want to run afoul the sheriff so I figured I needed to have a looksee to find out if there was any laws about poetry one way or the other.*

*I won't tell you all my adventures because there were too many and most of them weren't really worth the telling, but I saw a fair bit of Dallas and Houston and even El Paso on one occasion I'd just as soon forget.*

*It was in Austin, down in the fluorescent-lit subcommittee caverns beneath the capitol building, where I found my answers. I'd been walking around admiring all that pink granite and the grounds with all the fat squirrels and pigeons and lobbyists and all when I met an old guy mopping the floors after all the senators had left. He's the one who told me these poems I'm about to share.*

*He said he found them. Now, I don't usually go in for poems people say they found, but these two I'm about to relate are the closest I ever come to finding any kind of answer. I guess you could say they were found twice.*

*He told me,* the Texas State Legislature said, "Let There Be Poetry."

*He told me it was all written down in a big old leather-bound book like the ones you might of seen witches reading their spells from in the movies. It was called* Texas Administrative Code,

*and if you turned those musty old pages over to*

Title 19, Part II, Subchapter C §110.31. English Language Arts and Reading, English I (One Credit), Beginning with School Year 2009-2010. (b)  Knowledge and skills. (3) Reading/Comprehension of Literary Text/

*you'd find it.*

*He closed his eyes and started reciting in a low whisper. He said it was*

**Poetry.**

Students understand,
make inferences

draw conclusions
about the structure

& elements of poetry,

provide evidence from text

to support their understanding.
students are expected to analyze

the effects
of diction

and imagery

(
controlling images,
figurative language,
understatement,
overstatement,
irony,
paradox
)

in poetry.

*He stopped saying his poem, and I stood there taking it all in for a long time. I could hear footsteps echoing through those marble corridors like the sound of generations of people coming up from their final resting places just to hear what this janitor was saying, but those footsteps were just regular folks going about their evening, leaving work, unaware that there was some poetry right there in the middle of all that law.*

*I told him it sounded like that about covered reading poems, but what about writing them. He nodded and told me all those powerful senators and legislators thought of that too and so he shared another one he found, but it was under some different subsections and letters and what have you.*

*This one was shorter, kind of like one of those Japanese poems that never got a title and tells you a lot without using very many words so you have a lot of things to think about and maybe don't know exactly what the writer meant.*

write a poem
using a variety of
poetic techniques

and a variety
of poetic forms

*He let it sink in a moment or two and smiled and kind of leaned on his mop a little and told me he might of left some parts out, some commas and conjunctions and parentheticals and whatnot.*

*I don't know. And I don't know if those were any good or not either, but it sounded something like what I might be looking for.*

*The next morning, I headed back toward home and didn't stop until I got there.*

# An Irish Blessing

*M. V. Montgomery*

*for my father*

May the Lord put you in a witness protection program where the Devil can't find you.
May you always find yourself in the flow of traffic, and may the slower drivers stay
the hell out of your way. May your hair remain red enough to refract harmful UV rays.
May your appetite be hearty and the waistband of your trousers slack. May there be
no household project to ever get the better of you. May you shit out the colon cancer
if it starts to grow back, and then may the doctors go broke trying to find anything else
wrong with you. May the church parishioners listen in rapt attention to your readings
and your grandchildren hear your stories without any fidgeting. May you grow just
absent-minded enough to forget cross words. May your buddies from Korea stay out
of the obituaries. May your partner be there to chide you if you start to become morbid.
May you find samples at every supermarket and long-lost treasures at every yard sale.
May your coffin be constructed of toothpicks from fine dinners you haven't yet eaten.
May winter cold melt in your breath. May the road ahead be soft enough for slippers,
and may the Good Lord reserve for you a fine pair of size thirteens.

# Urban Testimony

*Maroula Blades*

What are you gonna do for the black artist,
the one whose voice dwindles in the storm?
We are not silent by any means, just black.
Black get back, your talk is too big and loud,
but not cheap like the shoes I wear, so bear
the brunt of my sass, the persistent itching
of my tongue on the back of your mind,
let what you think is the devil's wayward word
turn and club some sense, yes sense.
Black, up in your face not with guns, words.
I'm nigger with a book not a poptheweasle gun.
Suck this; chew the black lip truth,
Remnants of storms, hardcore, steadfast words,
fast and furious, quick in effect, deadly in assault,
funky, but still wanting peace. Believe!
Brethren, let me hear you say, 'well.' Word for the fearless.

# Divinations

*Maureen Alsop*

Ouranomancy

Stasis in winter is your belief in a window. From it you see the black maple spackles a hospital's brick wall into aubergine. The glass of the window carries the yellow glaze of traffic, the whorl of crimson wing tips, the slop of salt-water. Up high in the elms, light disappears, the bark of a bird dips among the red thrash of leaves.

The voice of three ships circle the harbor. Where a small house on the shore is made real by the sun. That you would bury your song. That you would go keyless into the sound of locks. That you were not human. That there would be no one to ask. But that you needed to ask in order to live.

Trucks excite grasses over the field. The skulls of unnamed birds lay scattered through mulberry. Ravens nest in the plum blossom. There is a ticking in the mind that thorns and unfurls into thistle. You still struggle but do not see what's gone. Capturing no hand you pray in fear you don't want to tell of your god-approximate to whom nothing is spoken... You invite the rain   bear scat   egg peel of nut hatch. Once   you ask yourself why stumble. Ask yourself   gentle   why laugh. You're not special. You're not not special. A worn thing. Falls here all around you. There is no comfort in language. Real words are soundless. But you gather no words.

Sometimes you believe you still hear him. But when you speak of his voice you close the window to the ocean for the last time.

Hydromancy

She will not hear snowflakes wild splatter into the strewn patches of cord grass. Winter's muck along the pond's edge, a mix of fawn tracks and duck droppings, freezes under the long white lines of her legs. There will be a twinge in her upper spine. There will be wet black flames drying in her braids. She moves through this air that is stunned by her heat. She regrets the passing of light, her Coppertone lathered face gleams like gold leaf. Her grandmother's wedding ring, now a spiral of seeds, pinwheels her marrow. Fractured spindles know no other cheek to kiss. Weathered witness, have courage. The coffee on the nightstand remains a clammy taste of seawater. She has spliced the last of her father's voice on the phone, three nights before his death, with the first bloom of yarrow. Her dusk phrases have buried all the songbirds. But the brine white hills will not blind. She opens each unfamiliar door between offerings. And lets there be no after thought.

Geomancy

Tonight an artist disemboweled a 100 year old Milton Piano. He thinks he is of the
'Pianist' tribe; a Native American tribe name given not to themselves, but designated men
who smashed their pianos into dust as they headed west. I listened to the last songs of the
yellow notes float, not into the sound of weeping, but into a room where branches of lin-
den oaks covered the walls. A boat overturns into the ironweed thicket. A dock lies buried
under mustard rows. A horse stumbles in inches of water brown as beer bottle. Unnamed
blood lily. At dawn I wish my neighbor's window unto an eastern lake. Accordingly, the
sun thins the afternoon into silent declaration.


Chiromancy

Someone spills water over your hand. Tonight the bridge will be sawed in half. Under
the guise of raw wood, your immaculate room shines. Under no sun. Gilt stones fill the
thorax. Under the beams grow weeds, grow fever. Rainwater errata Under the problem of
phones, because mostly there are none. Under the planks of the splintered dock your car
keys swim the harbor. Under your keel shaped sternum. Piles of medallions and crosses
bloat the thrift shop. The clovers repeat a swell of bees. Under the press of a wet night-
shirt's gauze. Under the red palm. Lady, your gold threads are slashes. Under the touch of
an old lover. Under the sparrows stain. Under the memory of the message that filled an
entire tape on your answering machine. Geranium florets blossom your breasts. The deep
white seams of you, space between lanterns.


Thumomancy

Soul, most recent of animals, your lost papers fill the closet. I would not notice your
soft intrusion. But for the vignette edge of the landscape, where your face is an accident
without origin. I see you have been here all along. Let me tell you, things can happen in
the years. Last winter a squirrel died in the cabin chimney. There is no single script. Only
the last of three orders of breath made before silence. Night has given me my wide addic-
tion. Under uncertain laws, in the sleep of no choice, I follow motivations downward into
the sweep of your pen. Scrawled lights of a new city wink between rows of tamarisk. The
center of the book is a catastrophe, but with love there is a lack of distance. You have led
me into the first threshold of your vision. Jupiter glows through a ragweed thicket. There
is no body. No sound. You go on without calculation for the beginning. You go on under
the lowering of gravity. Tonight the oncoming boxcar whistles your unfolding music.

# Eski Cami (Old Mosque)

*Elizabeth Angell*

1. The word *wahid* ("one") is superimposed over *Allah* (in outline only), so that together the composition can be read as "God is one."

2. *Hu*, or "He," meaning God.

3. Negative-space calligraphy (detail).

4. A doubled *waw*. The word *wa* means "and," and in this context signifies union.

5. Mirror calligraphy on a pillar.

6. A large *Allah* (with praying man as punctuation mark).

# The Atheist's Art of Prayer

*Caitlin Gildrien*

it was the day
my oldest friend left
for war

that i began learning
the atheist's art
of prayer.

having no-one to speak to,
I don't.
    —no pleas,
    no bargians
    (my good behavior
    for her life)
    and no hope that I might be heard—

just the bright burning in my heart,
my hands clasped tight to contain it,

    —while across the world
    she speaks in tongues
    and loses weight steadily, rapidly,
    until in her photos I can see only her skeleton
    peering through the face I used to know—

just my legs, buckled beneath me
and knees bruised
at the weight of it,

    —no favors,
    no reasoning,
    and no hope that I might be heard—

just the insensate laws of cause
and effect, of motion and time and chance,

just the desperate,
helpless, and involuntary feeling
of *please.*

# Faggot

*Dustin Brookshire*

I own the word
like you own your name,
let it roll off my tongue
and grate you like cheese.
Faggot.
Yes, I said it.
You're not deaf.
I don't stutter.
It's the word you want
to use against me,
pour over my body
like boiling water.
Baby, I can stand the heat.
It's a word
I once used.
Anthony. Faggot.
Brian. Faggot.
Lamar. Faggot.
It even tried to haunt:
Dustin. Faggot.
But I,
I deal the word
like a shark in Vegas.

# A quick visit to Joaquín's, and a ceremony

*Nathan Horowitz*

from *A Field Guide to Psychotropical Rainforest Birds*

January 15, 2007

It was the weekend, and my young students had received a solid week of English, so I caught a ride down the river to go see Joaquín at his hut. A visitor was there, Jim Timothy from California. In his early 40s, he was slim and in very good shape. He had a receding hairline and a pencil-thin moustache like John Waters. He boasted of his ability to dance as many hours as boyfriends half his age. He described himself as an urban shaman and an organizer of rave parties with a spiritual focus.

"We always have a chill-out room," he told me, "where there are always people on ecstasy having mellow conversations and giving each other backrubs. It's better than having them out on the street drinking and fighting."

He told me a dream in which he was in a natural history museum. In a dimly-lit corridor in the Egyptian section, he saw a diorama with a sphinx in it. She was alive and looking out at him through the glass. As he looked in her eyes he found that he was simultaneously himself and her, but more her than himself, because he was an emanation of her.

One day when he was a kid in Catholic school, he asked the priest, "We're supposed to love our enemies, right?"

"That's right."

"And the devil is our enemy, so we're supposed to love the devil, right?"

In another story he tells, he's way out in the desert on an Indian reservation in the southwestern United States after having eaten peyote. He's alone, naked, and playing a drum. A cloud of dust appears in the distance, gets closer. It's from an approaching car. The car keeps getting closer and closer. It's one of the tribal police cars. It drives up to him and stops. A big Indian cop wearing mirrored sunglasses gets out. Walks slowly up to him and says:

"You know you can't do this."

Jim says, "Yes."

The cop says, "All right," turns around, gets back in his car and drives away.

"Myths are computer chips," Jim remarked in another conversation, "concentrated intelligence, survival information for hard times."

---

I said, "One of my creative writing professors gave me a book of poems by the Serbian poet Vasko Popa called *Homage to the Lame Wolf,* named after an old Serbian tribal god. I found these poems astonishing because Popa was really operating from a different frame of reference than the other poets I was reading. The poems really were praise poems to this pagan god. I went to my professor and said this. He leaned back in his chair and said, 'Vasko Popa knows a lot about wolves.' I said, 'Like what?' My professor said, 'And his grandmother knew even more.' I said, 'Like what?' My professor said, 'How to make love to them.'"

Jim replied, "This is a story about someone I don't know well personally. We have a friend in common. This man works at an aquarium. They released one of their male sea lions back into the ocean. This man drives his car to the beach every Friday and picks up the sea lion and takes him home. He keeps him in the bathtub and feeds him fish, and they make love. On Sunday he returns him to the ocean."

Joaquín made a ceremony with Jim and me. He chanted over cups of yagé and we drank and settled into hammocks and relaxed. For a long time we were quiet, listening to insects chittering and tweeting, and frogs honking and groaning, a thrilling music of weirdness. My mind took off and crash-landed in a realm of fragrant, burnt language, where mumbo jumbo, gibberish, and gobbledygook reigned.

*Yagé's not a bug or a slug, it's a drug, but it's way more than that, it's a bat like a cat. It's the distillation of the echo of gunflower elves. It's green water in white rivers of blue oceans in the veins of bamboo. It's subcutaneous calico lichen, vibrating neon gum that chews itself against the teeth of your mind, it's an apparition of the face of Pan on a flower tortilla, it's yellow blades of sunlight magnified by the black earth, orange skeins of spunlight delighting us through the perfect planet, red dreams of the One Light shaking us gently in the midnight morning saying "Hey, old friend, wake up, it's time to BE, buddy. Time to be." (Be, be, be, be, be, the verb reverberates off my lips.)*

In a memory from my junior year in college, I'm lying on my back beneath a maple tree in October, blue sky above, and the intermittent cold breeze is shaking down the fantastic yellow red orange leaves, spinning against the sky as they fall. And I was thinking, "The tree is a natural clock that tells the time of the season. Each leaf that falls is another season second."

What are the ramifications of this?

I chant silently, many times, the name of Avalokitesvara, the bodhisattva of compassion.

I'm in a sub-aquatic realm of blue and green... there's something fierce about it... and it has many lizard eyes peering around. What I'm looking at is the fabric of lizard skins, and some gnomes in a workshop are cutting into it with instruments like cookie cutters, taking out lizard-shaped skins and sewing them onto lizard bodies. Of course lizards come into being through biological reproduction, I know that, but the natural process is mirrored by this supernatural one. This is simply how they fabricate lizards. The scene winks out and I'm in darkness again listening to the insect songs. Joaquín is snoring quietly.

---

I want to get rich selling fake wisdom, now that I know everything is fake. But then even my wealth will be fake, like Monopoly money. Sun, moon, and stars, all artificial—constructed like a stage set by elves attempting to convince us that this so-called reality is real. It's built by the elves of Maya, by Maya's elves, by My'selves—…. In this me-istic miasma of cells and selves, this self-same magnetic magma that is the body on yagé again. I'm in one of those places where everything one thinks of is true. So totally, undeniably accurate, and yet elsewhere it could be false. Truths have physical boundaries as much as countries have. I hold still, listening. Here the shamanic universe is infinitely vast and real. Elsewhere, it is not real, and other rules apply. And always, here, the crickets are singing, and my lungs are drinking this rich, clean air like a distillation of life itself.

More than yagé, I'm intoxicated by this divine, fragrant language of nature that keeps breathing within me and without me; I'm drunk on this plant animal language of squawks and whistles and humming and singing. An immense wave of nausea hits me, immediately followed by self-pity as I remember I will die someday, and then compassion as I remember everyone else will die someday too. With tears in my eyes I resign myself to pain, foreshadower of death.

And the crickets play their wordless songs with more intensity now, and I'm not sure whether the music is inside me or outside me, a language that reverberates through me until it's all that I am…. And I stretch and shift, relieving a pressure in my back, and float once again in the delicate black water of the forest night, my head clear, resigned to nausea and to the lightness of my limbs as if I were the captain of a boat sailing through a calm sky of smoke high above a burning city. I'm cold, and I pull the light blanket up around my shoulders. What are Jim and Joaquín doing? Go slow, my soul. My stomach hurts; I listen. Joaquín is again snoring quietly.

I recall a line from an early explorer's description of yagé customs: "Transported by the drink, the Indians dreamed a thousand absurdities and believed them as if they were true." Yes, how compelling these absurdities are! It's so easy to be transported by them! It's like you never knew you were a sailboat, and then the wind comes, and off you go! We drink a thousand truths and believe them as if they were dreams. We dream of the myths of man and the dreams we learn to believe in when we're dreamed into this world—night and day, something and nothing, here and there, now and then. We're all tiny shoots of the human plant, reified and pulsating.

Dozens of gnomes march past me in the darkness carrying strange tools. Fireworks explode behind them. Transported by the drink, I'm borne into a 4th of July memory from when I was a kid. It's 1974, I'm six years old, my mom and stepfather take me to the fireworks display at Veterans Park. They greet an aquaintance, Stacy, then move to an open space and spread out the secondhand quilt on which old automobiles are printed. My mom remarks about Stacy, "She's high as a kite." The display begins. I love the huge firecrackers booming in the drunken velvety summer sky, the whistling-screaming yellowy-white fireworks that corkscrew as they fall, the huge green plantlike ones that hold still in the high air with their smoke lit up by their fire, and the blue starlike ones that seem like love messages from outer space, while the spectators lie on blankets underneath, saying *Oooooo! Ahhhhh!* In 1996, I breathe deeply, living in two times, appreciating the old familiar glorious beauty.

Nausea.

Eagles and stars whirl around my vision, arrows and olive branches, stars and stripes, red, white and blue. This is part of my design. We're woven into each other. This is part of my totem pole. America the beautiful.

Nausea, increasing the beauty of the visions. My eyes run with tears: red, white and blue.

Nearby, in his hammock, my fellow American Jim Timothy clears his throat and sings, his voice ringing out like a bell in the darkness:

*The creator is our savior,*
*Hey ney yo wey,*
*The creator is our savior,*
*Hey ney yo wey.*

*Take care of us, take care of us,*
*Hey ney yo wey,*
*Take care of us, take care of us,*
*Hey ney yo wey.*

*The creator is our savior,*
*Hey ney yo wey,*
*The creator is our savior,*
*Hey ney yo wey.*

*Take pity on us, take pity on us,*
*Hey ney yo wey,*
*Take pity on us, take pity on us,*
*Hey ney yo wey.*

*The creator is our savior,*
*Hey ney yo wey,*
*The creator is our savior,*
*Hey ney yo wey.*

# The Names of the Dead are Floated to Heaven, Gyeongju, South Korea

*Robin Susanto*

# (incantation: ekstatic)

*Jeneva Stone*

I have gone back to ground
back to the fine root hairs
that lie along your skin

gone back to ground I have
in hand the world's blue cup
faint musk of you within

back to ground I have gone
into murk of natal flesh
thrust of the child-wish

gone to ground for you I yearn
bound to you ever make return

# November

*cin salach*

*Spell for the Undoing of Prayers*

*Let go the hands that fold me, let go the tongue that tells me*
       *the trees the creek, they know, they will speak me now*

*Let go the house that holds me, let go the family that calls me*
       *the moon the sun, they know, they will hear me now*

*Let go the name that follows me, let go the voice that carries me*
       *the ocean the stones, they know, they will sing me now*

*Let go the sex that begins me, let go the veil that becomes me*
       *the ground the breeze, they know, they will reveal me now*


\*


I leave     my signs of leaving spread neatly across the floor     announcing
    *I'm leaving*

    to architect my own body

in the smooth ache of arch and bridge    the red belly of fly and seed    green of water
gold of wind    stillness of pine and stone    crawl of light.

    *I'm leaving*
                to hear my own body answer:

    she is a wave, all the rest is negotiable.

# A Language of One

*Allen C. Fischer*

He uttered
tainted ellipses,
guttural sounds
empty of syllable
so his words
were other than
I had ever heard.
His yaw, jive and
garble mimicked,
it seemed,
a marred parrot.

Seated in the back
corner of the
subway car, he
was in continuous
self-rejoinder,
chortling,
purling, braying.
Everyone else
out of it.
We locked glances
as though at any

moment, madness
might commit fury
and send us
running for our lives.
But the man
paid scant attention
to us as he followed
the thread of his
conversation,
come 2nd Avenue,
out of the car.

# ARKEO 4

*Marja-Leena Rathje*

archival inkjet and collagraph on paper
81 x 61 cm. (32" x 24")

# The Charmed Life

*Susannah Rich*


It takes nothing — talent nor courage —
to be a sleeping princess
in a house of glass — Tiffany doves
floating in door lights, gold

-camed windows, panes that mirror
interior lights over outer darkness.
Things break only from others' use —
etched flutes and tumblers; the crystal

witch's ball hung to ward off evil;
Murano lamps; silvered walls;
the central vacuum...
Glaziers come, like charioteers,

with ladders and Unrue racks
to unscrew old strike plates, bleed
the furnace, crawl on their bellies
amongst toads and kittens

transparent in the walls. This is living
in the sky, in the full neon of the sun,
glitter of stars, a store of Magic
Ginger Ale — phosphate bubbles

unreleased — the aspic mold of pansies,
the heart-shaped ice cubes for guests
who bear their envy, to the altar
of you... For a spell to be a spell,

it must be broken — the rescuer must be
disguised, the rescued must seem to sleep
in a life of liquid suspense — perfect,
cold — waiting to be shattered...

# Islam for Americans

*Khadija Anderson*

1. means god in Arabic

      99 names

no eyes
no ears

Al lah
Al lah

      AL LAH

alif lam lam alif

Allah is not male
NOT male

not a man
or he
or HE

or anything that
you

can imagine


2. Does your husband make you wear that?

I am a
wrapped piece
of candy a
swaddled jewel
I am perfect
woman under
my packaging
you may not see
my effusive gold mahr
my fruitful awrah

---

3. Does your religion make you wear that?

the woman
who does not
cover her hair
should have it
shorn
~ Corinthians 15:6


4. Tessellation

Middle Eastern Art Scheherazade veil sheikh
The Alhambra calligraphy Afghanistan burqa
Palestine hashish Morocco pyramids violence
hooknosed Arabic sword mosque haram thief
sand nigger Sinbad jihad camel whore infidel
Iraq belly dancing terrorist Aladdin barbarian
Sahara couscous hookah Rumi rag head bitch


5. last words

I see a woman covered
in a long dress, headscarf
and face veil
salaam aleykum, I say
and as she looks at my
bare head, tank top
and tattoos
she replies,
wa aleykum salaam sister

# Pomegranate

*Maya Massar*

So ripe
I cannot eat it
With any semblance
Of politeness

Gory with its black-red juice
I am an animal

Vibrant with the naked hunt
Lush with the kill

I return to the prayer of ancestors

Mother of the Cave
Make me your witness:
I am She who Lives

Pomegranate

Too bloody for the rest

Has saved my life

Amen.

# Unenforceable Promise

*Julia Martin*

The party of the first part
to this most personal service contract —
departed

Scratch that clause
on successors and assigns

Our vow to love forever?
Void *ab initio*
per the statute of frauds

Not to impugn or imply
a deceptive intent

The existence of mutual mistake
— a flaw in formation —
is not material

yet loop-de-loops
through my head

A closed track clacks and shuttles
an infinitely regressive plea
v. renvoi

# Elements of Force

*Karyn Eisler*

Clouds    Lightning

Wind     Rain

# How I Would Do It

*Angela Just*

*on seeing my baby picture in an album*

Come here and be my child. I will force-feed
you to fatness: nothing denied — and everything
that was. Cram it all down your throat.

(You will write it later, of course, my meanness
and my kindness, the teeter-totter you'll call mother.)

How roly-poly a baby, your face buried in the cake and frosting
of nursery rhymes. Start you on Emily at six and hide
Sharon Olds under the bed for your adolescent consumption.

I will take you to the deep forest and leave you
without breadcrumbs to take communion
with weeds and berries, the sap of maple trees.
There among rooted things you will forage for the roots
of words, dark etymologies for the poems to come.

I'll plant memory chips the size of poppy seeds
behind your ears so you can find your way back
to all you will read and touch — nothing
will escape you. In this way you will grow large.

At night your arms will accept the slow drip
of world mythology and baseball, biology
and quantum physics. Thus, time is saved for practice
of three instruments: piano, cello, and your own voice.
Especially your own voice.

And when your eyes are bulging and your ears
grow like cabbages, when your teeth are working
overtime in your full mouth and your greedy pores
binge on whatever the air brings, then we will see
what you do with this excess of flesh and blood. Choose
starvation if you will. My work is done: I leave you

with a full larder and a root cellar
that will never lack for words.

# Man Date

*Penn Kemp*

House. Hold. Man. Age. Meant.
Well. Well, whoever would have

guessed? Not me, when I was up
and away, running and running off

steam, that I'd return to a house to run,
the one I ran from forty-odd years back.

Now resounding, rolling round and
round the block, the wo(r)ld follows,

shouting curses, blessings, woundings,
winding me back here where I began.

Only courage lets me remain, lets me rest,
to maintain the stiff demeanour of brick

veneer by which I was raised. Rest and all
the rest is easy always. Words to swear by,

words to return here, open-handed. Home.

# The Mist in Morning

*Barbara LaMorticella*

Let everyone on earth who is alone now
reading, sleeping, sitting in small rooms
alone and meditating,
cutting wood, walking desperately through
dark nights

Let everyone alone and praying
Let everyone alone and grieving
Let everyone alone

Let everyone contained and pure
in solitude know — Know

That in the early morning hours
all the prayers of solitaries
rise vibrating out of the dim earth,
not like birds but like
the deepest voice of earth itself

Rise out of the tangled grasses
of individual living
the way the mist does in the morning —
softly, surely,

Reclaiming and replenishing heaven.

# The Butcher's Wife's Tale

*Colleen McKee*

His heart was a poppy, paper-thin.
From the women's balcony I heard it
during the silent prayers.
His shoulderblades trembled under his tsallit, weapons
I wanted for myself. Blame it on Lilith,
on boredom. Blame it on dirt
got into the mikveh. Blame it
on my red hair, or the gap between
my front teeth, which is a sign
of lustfulness in women, or at least distracts men
from my lack of beauty. But on what
shall I blame love? I asked him
to bring me a loaf of challah,
made in his mother's kitchen.
I was his first. It was easy from there.

The rebbe's son, I would meet him
a bit before dawn, holding a lamp,
the cellar door barely open.
Koomt tsoo mir — my hand in the door,
pulling him in, under the earth
fragrant with apples. We kissed
in the darkness of apples.

Upstairs, we smoked cigarettes, and the last of the night
clung to our skin: the dark gold of tobacco,
red gold of his hair, the silver of moon
and of smoke. Our picnics in the garden
of my hand-embroidered bed. A few braids of challah,
the twice-blessed wine, the spiciest
wursts, slaughtered and stuffed by
my husband's callused hands.
On the trousseau, a half-eaten apple
bruised red to gold.

How could I do it? you wonder,
soft and snug before dawn,
as my husband fed cows
from bare hands? I did it because
of my husband's hands, because
they were twice as big as my own, animal-
grizzled and freckled and red, pushing
me down and inside me, pushing

beyond what I had. Understand, he was
what I wanted. But then, I wanted a pet of my own. I wanted
white skin of my own to whip,
to kiss and surprise, to bind.

We'd smoke my husband's cigarettes, rolled
between his thick fingers, pilfered
from his gold case. One morning,
(my husband in Chelm to see about buying a goat)
we woke late to embroidered sheets smeared with ash,
dirty vines on the hem of the bed,
gray pomegranates where we laid our heads.
A dusting of ashes covered the floor —
my lover was the first to notice
the tracks in the ash, like a bird's,
but the size of a woman's foot. And the lid
was off my jewelry box, my necklaces scattered
in front of the mirror. Who had been trying them on?
My husband's gold cigarette case
was newly engraved with some letters — Hebrew —
I cannot read — when I asked what they said,
my lover just clutched at his curls and wept.
Dybbuk, dybbuk, he muttered. Lilim, lilim, ach…
He drew diagrams in dust with his fingers
as I pulled up my stockings and braided my hair.
He told me to hide the cigarette case.
I dropped it in the well, watched the gold
Flash in the sun and the water.
There were spots in my eyes all day.
I told my husband it was an accident.

Today, the rebbe's son barely looks up from his books
when I buy bread from his mother.
Every morning there's a sea in my belly.
I can't bear the salt sweat
beneath my swollen breasts, or the scent
of meat, though my husband makes me eat it,
for the child, he says, for the roses
in my cheeks. He hopes for a boy
and is happy, but I know it will be
a girl like me, that the restlessness
I bear inside me will beat
in her poppy-thin heart. For her I won't bother
with ribbons, red ribbons in my hair,
or hers, in the doorway, the bars
of her cradle. I will name her after me. Everyone
will whisper, How can she do such a thing?

The Angel of Death is not so smart.
When he comes to your house, two with one name,
he won't know who to take.

I am an animal, an animal in love.
Love is lodged in the muscle, the best cuts
of meat. Fire cannot wash love away, nor
can salt scour it clean.
Of ashes will always be embers.

When my daughter is born, I will hold her,
glistening red. I will kiss
her pink hands, her gold curls.
I will call her a shayne maidl.
I no longer fear
the evil eye.
I will take her
to the well, toss
my gold bracelets in first.
When she reaches for them,
I'll give her a push.
All day long, I know,
I will be punished
by spots in my eyes
from her gold curls
flashing in the sun as she falls.
When they ask, I will say,
It was an accident.
Because, in a way, it was.

# Afterthought

*Steve Wing*

# Tricks

*Zoe Polach*

We had a list of all the things that were important. It was a long list, but not too long, because it was very carefully edited. *Thrift* was on it, and *wearing pants*, and so was *keeping good records*. We'd made too many mistakes to forget that one.

One day at the end of winter, we were debating over lunch whether we should add something to the list. In the middle of the discussion, a stranger wandered in. We asked her what her name was, where did she come from, but she just smiled and asked politely if there was enough to share. We said, of course there is (*hospitality* was #14), pull up a chair and help yourself.

We continued talking, and the stranger listened attentively. At the end of the meal she thanked us for our kindness. She was a wandering magician, and she wondered if she might pay us back by putting on a little show. We said, we love a good magic trick, what've you got?

With great ceremony she pulled out a deck of cards. They were bigger than your average playing cards, and we thought they had different pictures, but we couldn't quite make them out.

After shuffling them with all kinds of fancy flicks of the wrist, she fanned the cards out face-down and offered them to the nearest person. Take one, she said. He did, and turned it over. It read, simply, #20: *paying debts*. He read it out loud, and everyone looked at each other.

The magician took the card back. This is my best trick, she said, proud and a little shy. She traced the letters on the card with one long finger and they disappeared under her touch.

We wanted to be polite, but we didn't understand. She said, you'll see it if you try again. This time the card read #14: *hospitality*. As the word dissolved we felt something, a feeling whose name we couldn't remember. Maybe we'd better see it again, we said, sitting up in our seats.

We erased our portraits, too, and our mortgages, and lots of things that people believed in. And every entry on our list had gone up in smoke before we were done. We felt better than we had in years.

When we were finished, we told her that after all this, we had to know her name. She said, I forget, I'm sorry, was it important?

# He Gives Me My Nahuatl Name

*Susan Elbe*

*for Francisco Alarcón*
*August 7, 1994*

I, myself am not bird,
my bones, not hollow
easy flutes for song.

I, myself am not snake,
my skin not silver
husk that sloughs me new.

But I, myself am the green
voice jabbering
down the fields. My palms

push sky, reek of sun
and I cadence
the night with whispering.

I, myself take to ice, brittle
with rime, shimmy
in dry wind — *chicome, chicome.*

*Note: Chicome is the Nahuatl numeral 7. In Aztec mythology, Chicomecoatl ("Seven Snakes") was the Aztec goddess of maize. She is sometimes called Goddess of Nourishment, a deity of plenty and the female aspect of corn. Her symbol is an ear of corn. Source: Francisco X. Alarcón. Other sources say that Centeotl, the Corn God, is the provider of the Spirit Soul (Teyollia) for days with the numeral 7 (chicome). There is a lot of crossover between Nahuatl and Aztec mythology.*

# I am waiting for the right instant to say your name

*Peg Duthie*

I have torched battalions of straw men
in my quest to spin an ending to my liking.
I have cajoled seeds into uprooting secrets
before they are even drowned or buried.
I have fleeced both witches and sailors
and clothed empresses with newsprint veils.
I have given nothing away, although
many who partake of my measures fail
to recognize that everything bears a price.
I learned this from you. Your prints form a ghost
under everything I touch, a phantom
under every map I sketch, and once
I cease to care about what left's to lose, I
will free you from the lump lodged in my throat.

## The Killer Poem

*Paul Stevens*

One day I'll write a poem so wild
    It will knock you off your perch!
You'll pick yourself up from the floor
    Weak-kneed and cross-eyed, lurch

Towards me wailing, 'I must have
    That poet — give him to me!'
See, that's why I write and write
    And write this poetry.

# Bird Transformation

*Harvey Parker*

# The Taut String

*Joe Hyam*

Put your ear to the hollow stone and see if you can hear,
In the corners of the town or in the dark and lonely house,
In the country of your head, where unstoppable rivers flow,
The childrens' prayer that you trust no more, but can't forget,
In the nursery of the rhymes that break upon your sleep.

For you may fear the hidden voice that only the dead can hear
And the shapes that change and chatter in the cave of sleep,
The words repeated, counted off like beads, lest you forget,
Where in the country in your head, tides of reason ebb and flow
And flood the foundations and secret places of the house.

Words winged with messages so cruel you struggle to forget,
That multiply with tiny feet and gnaw the timbers of the house,
That destroy, with spells and curses, the precious cave of sleep,
That cackle in your ears all night to make sure that you hear
The cries of people drowning in the headlong rivers' flow.

Cup your ear, though, to the stone, in case you should forget
Kind words that open and close, like magic, the doors of your house,
And promise treasures and relief, bring calmness to the rivers' flow,
Its provenance and destiny in the estuaries of sleep
Where whispered words come and go, sometimes, too soft to hear.

"Ring a ling" the voices go with spells and riddles through the house,
What they mean you do not know, but still they flow as rivers flow,
Down in the dark, where it is cold and, therefore, you must forget,
The whispers and promises of love; or you will never sleep,
The whispers which you cannot trust, and dare no longer hear,

But dread, for they wander free like burglars in the house.
Whatever are they looking for? What do they want while you sleep?
They move the furniture and dance to music which you cannot hear.
Stand tiptoe and pirouette and hope that you'll forget
How fast, how cold, how unstoppable is the rivers' flow.

Again and again, in the same order, the same words, you hear,
In the stone, in the taut string, in the timbers of the house,
Carousing in your head where the tides of reason ebb and flow.

# Looking for an Oracle

*Amy MacLennan*

Spool it on out for me: where to turn left,
the bananas to pick, the men to catch,
the men to ditch, tell me when my nails
will break and the roof will fail,
tip me to gossips and scratched-out phone book names,
list out my losses (hearing gone in ten years,
the loves I'll bury),
line them up so I can swallow them all
without the coil of worry –
choice never stopped the clots in anyone's veins
or the smooth sky pressing down,
and I want my days laid flat,
my facts splayed out, a plan, a map,
to the last damn chicken bone
that sticks in my throat.

# Directions' Introduction

*Francis Raven*

How to despise a word
so much you inscribe
it on your forehead every night
before going out to the bars
so you won't have to say it.
How to hide behind a sign.
And then, how just to hide.
How to despise a word
so much that when uttered
you immediately need a gimlet.
How to hate a word so much
you write it on thousands of pieces
of construction paper
and rip them up
while watching reruns of Friends.
How to surreptitiously cut
your word out of every dictionary
at your "neighborhood" Borders.
How to burn a word anyway.
How to laugh inappropriately and off-key
when anyone intones it.
How to change its meaning
by forming several on-campus focus groups.
How to still have it stab you.
How to kick its referent
around the block
so you wake with sore feet
and ripped shoelaces.

# Letters to My Father

*Marjorie Stamm Rosenfeld*

Each one had to be edited,
every ambiguous word excised.
How pungent words were!
My mother's eyes
traveled the page —
down, up, left, right,
regimenting each line.
Mustn't offend him.
Mustn't say
something he might mistake.
If I spoke of an ocean voyage,
described myself as putting out —
my God, I'd named myself a harlot!
I made promises, took oaths.
Oaths became curses
in the crinkles of his mind.
He was a wordsmith too. His hand —
the right one — blessed,
pulled its object close.
The sinister left one
drove the sculpting stiletto in.
After him, how could I trust
tenderness? The best he gave me
was when he called me a cat,
said if you dropped me
from the 7th story,
I'd land on my feet.
No small feat that!
Thanks, Dad, for my sense
of ambiguous language.
Thanks, even, for the thumps
on my wet clay that felt like blows.
Your hand crafting finished me.
I am your best poem.
Read me.

# The Blasphemer

*Carrie Ann Baade*

# Lullaby

*Sarah Burke*

Say goodnight to the wind and the trees,
apples flinching on the branch; say goodnight
to yourself. Let me lead you back to the well,

the origin, quiet dark you knew once
and forgot. Let me show you the first night
on earth, still happening, still haunting

old star charts buried in the dust, insects
trapped in bottles, embryonic jungles
pulsing under highways, whispering,

*let's rebuild   remake   stand up in our joy*
*let's dance the dream our feet remember*
*sing the dream our throats carried back*

*from the dead*   There comes a memory
of thorns, berry juice deep in the summer.
There comes a memory of letting go,

washing ankles under the cold white moon.
Remember I began in silence, star my mother
carried through peace and war as a child,

star among millions, chosen by chance
to twin without end, carry stars of my own.
I want a beginning deeper than birth,

deeper than history, to search my bones
for one syllable trembling with cosmic storms.
Forgive me. I've been terrible and sweet.

Let me forgive you. Let fall your curtains,
your clothes. Let in the wind and the trees again,
apples and branch again, let in the night.

## Toxic Cylinder

*Julene Tripp Weaver*

Mom, they want to bomb
holes in my aura,
they fucked our men at war:
    your husband, my father,
    your brother, my uncle.
They're bombing Iraqi children with plutonium.

Bumblebees can't hardly kiss nectar,
the world is awry.

I came a long way
    from bearing a child
my two-time denial scream
    then the ultimate screech,
    *No way Jose,*

we live in a toxic cylinder
where martyrs have
no good reason to live.

Not complacent, but I sit,
sip tea in my condo in America,
I have a man, a passport, a beater car.
A single white woman hanging onto a job
my nails scrape cement, but I carry on.

It's enough already, enough
    it's good, good enough
I breathe, pay my bills, stand on my head,
    have caller ID.

An all American white girl
    not complacent being fucked
        so they better leave me the fuck alone.

# For Tom W.—Eyes Only

*Linda Umans*

I never identified with the straight back **L**
or the manuscript loops    too girly maybe
(I'm way more loopy now)
the erectile **i** was a better fit
definite and pointing away
hanging on the dromedary **n**
riding    slow    rhythmic
the **d**    dropped stomach about to birth
(the late births knock me out)
enclosed   sometimes pampered in the space of the **a**
a place for a round girl to curl
the open-topped **U** a way up and out   but challenging
the **m** a human purr
another **a** when I need it again
the **n** this time connecting to the final **s**
my sign in China
an all-time hissing favorite.

I'd like my ashes
carried to the ocean
in Townes' flying shoes (you know)
(I've imagined it already
been there already
so if it's inconvenient…)

my true remains are yours.

# The Language of God

*Ayesha Saldanha*

To learn Arabic is to learn to speak of the divine. God enters every conversation, whether you intend Him to or not. Thanks be to God. If God wills. God's blessings upon you. May God give you health. Thank God for your safety. God be with you. God forbid. Only God knows.

To learn Arabic is to enter a world of formulas, expressions of the sacred, which frame life, its events and actions. Everything is rooted in His will. Formulas give every interaction a reassuring structure. Their repetition bestows power, reminds you that God is ever-present, central to all. Yet repetition can also remove meaning — for these are words it is impossible not to say.

To learn Arabic is to learn to introduce these formulas of the divine into your speech. And after Arabic has become part of your thoughts, has carved new patterns of language in your mind, when you speak English those formulas leave an echo in your conversations. Imagine sneezing, and not hearing 'Bless you.' It is that absence, magnified.

...

As I look at a copy of the Qur'an, the Arabic accompanied by the English 'interpretation' — for God's words are believed to be a miracle, inimitable, and impossible to translate — I see the Arabic words tightly curled, compact and potent. The English words sprawl loosely beside them. A word in the Qur'an can become two, three, four, five words, even a sentence, in English.

...

The recitation of a single letter of the Qur'an is considered a form of worship, and worthy of reward.

...

Twenty-nine of the Qur'an's chapters start with short sequences of letters, called *muqatta'at*. If their meaning was ever known to humankind, that knowledge has been lost, and scholars over the centuries have put forward various theories with no consensus reached. The one point of agreement is that only God knows the exact meaning of the *muqatta'at*.

*Alif Lam Ra. Alif Lam Mim. Ha Mim. Ta Sin. Ya Sin. Ta Ha.*

...

Baha'u'llah, founder of the Baha'i faith, which has its roots in Islam, wrote a commentary on the *muqatta'at*. In it he described God's creation of the Eternal Alif by the Primordial Pen. After being called by God to set down the mysteries of pre-existence upon the Perspicuous, Snow-White Tablet, the Pen was first stupefied by intense yearning for 70,000 years, then wept crimson tears for 70,000 years. Then, as it stood erect between the hands of God, a black teardrop fell from it upon the Tablet — and the Divine Point took on the form of the Eternal Alif.

...

In the beginning was —

# Bittersweet

*Christina Pacosz*

*Snow drifts on the Rocky Mountains*
*Buffalo herds*
*race across the ice*
*The wind blows*
*so strongly*
*as the sun fights its way*
*to a fresh new day*
      —Alton Fred Brown
      April 17, 1984 – April 10, 2001

Bitter-root
bitter cress
bitter-bloom
bitter weed
Bitter Gourd

Awash in bitterness
like moonlight
at forty below
midden heaps
beneath old city snow

Berries of Kansas hawthorn
smashed on sidewalks
or shat by birds
hungry in this drought
Bittersweet orange

Decades of mourning
a member of the family
Celastraceae
called Wahoo in the Audubon guide
An American tree
its powdered bark
a purgative
Purple berries
winter fare
for cardinals and chickadees

Death's inexorable plow
laying open furrow after furrow
of virgin prairie
Osage orange
eastern cedar
honey locust

The sad butchery
that buried him
on his seventeenth birthday
and before that his father
murdered
in front of his two-year-old eyes

Then dust and grit
March gusts pelt
the windshield with
almost two centuries later

Bitter-root
bitter cress
bitter weed
Bitter-bloom
bitter fruit
Bitter Gourd

Buffalo-ooooo-ooo
O   OOO  O oo o

# Dream

*Anne Morrison Smyth*

# A Warning

*Stuart Barnes*

Like kangaroos,
Cane toads or rabbits,
You can be eradicated,

Annihilated
With the flick of a finger,
The jellyfish-pulse of a thought.

Don't you forget —
This is *my* life.

# Common Needs

*Robin Chapman*

*for Jim Martyn*

My friend with ALS has moved to hospice.
Rick Steve's tours of Europe streaming
on the Mac, a mouse he can click with a toe.
cough machine at the ready, biPap mask
for extra breath, for sleep, a meal pureed
to soup consistency. Time, still,
for visits, paying taxes, but I'm looking
up communication boards for the time
when speech goes too — this one,
pared to thirty-three commands —

may there be thirty-three angels for Jim,
wings color-coded, jerseys numbered,
to be called in for specialty plays —
*moisten mouth, tighten mask,*
*move my thumbs, bring bed bath,*
*I'm hot, I'm cold;* angels of breathing,
angels of cough, angels of settling the pillow
under his head, his shoulders, his knees;
angels bearing the bedpan, diapers,
the urinal; and send the angel of attention
to watch his eyes, fixed on number 33,
summoning the angel of the call switch
to watch over sleep.

# A Widow's Curse

*Bev Wigney*

Let vultures tug at
the eyes and wallets
of the local yokels
who circle my farm
thinking I lost my brains
along with my husband,
and will sell out for a song
as I'm too dumb to know
what my land is worth.

May whining cicadas
jam up the ears of every
customer service rep
who said they'd change
an account over to my name
but never bothered so that
the monthly statements
continue to arrive addressed to
a dead man instead of me.

Let the Demons of Cosmos
break off manicured nails
and smear lipstick
on the face of any silly twit
who tugs on the arm of her mate,
towing him to safety,
after she discovers "her man" has been
chatting with a woman who (yikes!)
is revealed to be "a widow."

Send yellow-bellied sapsuckers
to peck and lick at the cowards
who called themselves
family and friends
but never visited my husband
during his illness
when he could have used
someone to talk with
other than me.

May I be showered with pennies
for every time a
well-meaning friend has blithely chirped:
"You're still young!
You'll find someone else!"
as though dead soulmates
could be replaced with as little regard
as a pair of worn out hiking boots
or a broken canoe paddle.

# Credere

*Dick Jones*

> *If God did not already exist, it would be necessary*
> *to invent him.* —Voltaire
> *"He's God, cried all the creatures…"*
> —James Thurber, "The Owl Who Was God"

If there has to be a God —
no option on the broken
road, the bridge of sighs —
then let it be a dancing god,

like Shiva but a voiceless one,
indifferent, treading out
the double loop, the bee's infinity
of weaving round and round until

the measure's known by all.
Or if not the dancer,
how about a singer?
One who cants in tongues,

a *lingua franca* from the
furnace heat (*ex corde vita*),
singing the blues, *sean nos*,
*la duende*, passionate, engaged,

yet powerless to lift the curse
of Sisyphus, or block the juggernaut,
or move the stone. These gods omnipotent,
who claim our praise and swallow

our prayers like hungry birds,
are dreams that draw
on the oxygen of our need.
We might as well worship

water falling, shape-shifting
clouds, the janus faces watching
from the cliffs that tell us
what we want to know.

# Emptiness

*Catherine Ednie*

There you are, absence, there you are, soothing, black, and gone, there you are, more quiet than the thin dark mushrooms rising in a circle on the lawn at night. I call you and I draw you down, draw you close.

Emptiness, emptiness, I lift your black host in my hands, in honor, arms tense. Fingers long and shaking, I stroke your lack of outline and smell your faintest odor of cold and rain and the divine. I enfold you in my hands — look there between the crevasses created by my thumbs — I see you, your dark honor and your dignity. I have you, emptiness, I take you every night to my room where you assist me. You snuff out the candles and croon no lullaby, blacken my eyes and take me silently to dreamless sleep.

# The Seven Healing Saints

*Lucy Kempton*

These photos were taken at the Chapel of Notre Dame du Hault, in Trédaniel, Côtes d'Armor, Brittany. It is the home of "Les Sept Saints Guérisseurs," the Seven Healing Saints, polychrome wood sculptures of uncertain age and provenance, each invested with the power to relieve certain afflictions.

The Saints are St Houarniaule (or Hervé), St Mamert, St Méen, Ste Eugenie, St Lubin, St Livertin, and St Hubert. They were called on to cure a range of common maladies, such as migraines, eye troubles, rheumatism, but also mental and psychological problems; blind St Houarniaule who traditionally kept a dog or perhaps a wolf who ate the dog and was commanded by the saint to take its place, on a leash, was invoked to help with fear and 'angoisse,' anxiety, to master the wolf in a more figurative sense. St Hubert helped with dog-bites and rabies, 'la rage,' so by extension with rage and fear, the connection between fear and anger preempting modern psychological understanding. Ste Eugenie is the only woman, but wasn't always; she was a feminised and Catholicised development of St Tujan, or Ujan, a much older, more indigenous saint, who was possibly in turn a Christianised version of a pre-Roman Celtic sun-deity.

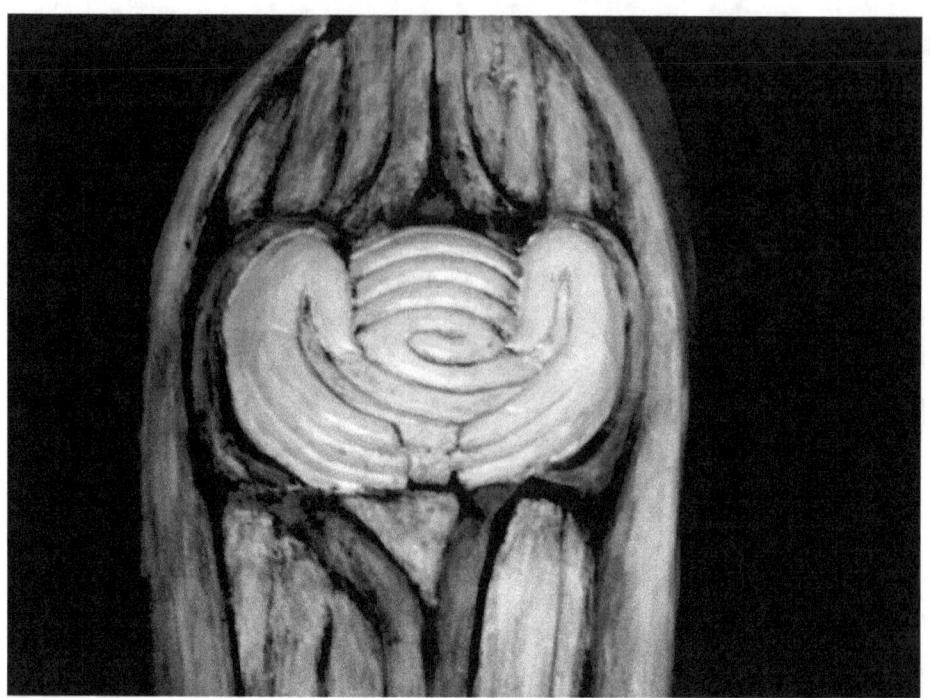

St Mamert looked after intestinal troubles, including colicky babies. His intestines are exposed, open, and he holds them tenderly, a rather pretty pink coil of gut, between his two hands.

For a long time people brought gifts and offerings, oblations, for the Saints' favours, either to propitiate or to thank them. They gave money, but also things like linen, hemp, butter, honey and beeswax, even piglets. The revenues from the chapel were enormous for such a small, out-of-the-way place. But by the end of the 19th century people began to offer other kinds of votives, these little plaques, mostly marble with engraved gilded lettering. They are in thanks for services rendered, and mostly simply say 'Merci,' Thank you, one or two are in English, some quite recent. (Many are also to Notre Dame to whom the Chapel is dedicated) The effect of the same word in different variations over and over in the gloom and candlelight is rather hypnotic.

Things have always made their way to the chapel, been sheltered by or given to it; the Saints' statues were not all always there, some were probably brought from another religious foundation, a leper hospital, at about the time of the Revolution. This relief carving is an enigma, was perhaps brought here in the mid-20th century during one of the chapel's periods of restoration from another demolished church or chapel. I always think of it as the angel with the book, but elsewhere the object is described as a blank escutcheon, a heraldic support for words or symbols. Book or shield, there is a feeling that the angel is bringing something of importance that should tell us something, but it can't be read.

Unfortunately, what drew wealth of course drew thieves, and the chapel was not infrequently robbed throughout its history. Then in the 1980s the Saints themselves were stolen. They were replaced by plaster copies, which were stolen again in the last few years. The statues in these photos are very new replicas of the originals, that have recently been installed.

They are faithful and sympathetic copies, the scale and forms and colours are all as they should be. But the idea of replacing the Saints is problematical; it's difficult to grasp how practical and concrete the kind of faith they were part of was. They weren't just representations of spiritual power, the power was the object. We see them as curious works of art, which might or might not house a spiritual reality, but that's not quite the point. The spiritual and material reality used to be one and the same. So making new ones to replace the old shouldn't work.

Unless the power is within the place, rather than its furniture and artifacts. This has always been a sacred place, a place of healing; the chapel and the Saints are quite recent emanations of this. If you walk west from the chapel, past some prehistoric standing stones, into a wooded ravine, you'll come to the holy well. In mediaeval times it was dedicated to St Tujan, and has been a sacred place probably since the bronze age; Gallo-Roman remains have certainly been found there. People throw the age-old votive offerings of coins into the well. There is a stone cross and other stone artefacts from who know where set up here. A fallen tree covered in ivy forms an arch in front of it. On the ivy stems someone has inscribed the words 'Cécile tu nous manques' — 'Cécile we miss you.'

Who knows who Cecile is or was and why she is missed, but someone brought their sadness, their *angoisse* to this particular place of power and left it as an offering in these words, a poignant counterpoint to the marble plaques of gratitude.

*With thanks to Bertrand L'Hôtellier for help with the research on the chapel of Notre Dame du Hault.*

# Self-Portrait as Dryad, No. 7

*Marly Youmans*

The golden haze around these whips of limbs
Is glistening, awakening to light
Within retreating clouds — embattled fire
That melts the snow and pellmell sends the sky
To run in ditches near the highway's edge.

My God, I am no witch to suffer so —
Who tied me to this stake that frosts my skin?
Who makes me tremble with his solar heat?
Who takes my voice and shakes the syllables
Until I speak in otherworldly tongues?

Dear Christ, the world is aching in its grave,
And can I bear another spring-time thaw?
O Willow, Willow, I uncurl to let
The bite and simmer of this raking gold
Explode in leaves — green eyes that weep for me,
My harrowed hell, my star-enkindled tree.

# Trance

*O Thiam Chin*

The old man arrived at the kampong much earlier than expected. He had walked for an hour to reach where we stayed, and by the time he stepped foot into the house, he was perspiring all over. My grandfather and uncles were told that he was the most revered medium in the district, one who could summon and talk to any spirit he wanted to, to ask a request or favour, or to seek blessings or placation; his services available for a small token amount of 'coffee money.' To me, he was just like any old man — severe, toughened, wrinkled.

My mother told me to serve him a cup of coffee, and when I brought it to him, he gave me a White-Rabbit sweet in return. Then he turned back to my grandfather, his countenance serious, and continued with their discussion. I only caught a few snatches of words, before running out of the house, to join my other cousins at play, the sweet already melting in the heat of my palm.

That night, the old man stayed for dinner and ate at the table with the men of the family. Their heads remained lowered in deep talk, and the old man closed his eyes while he listened.

The wooden sedan-chair was brought in from the storage hut and placed before the altar that was ladled with food offerings and urns burning with smoky, eye-burning incense. The painted faces of the warrior gods and benevolent goddesses flickered with numerous changes of expression as the flames from the candles shuddered with each rotation of the overhead fans. We, the children, were told not to go into the living room for the night, or linger outside the corridor. We had to keep away from the procession.

But we watched nonetheless, peeking from behind tiny slits in the paneled doors, taking turns to observe the goings-on in the room. The old man had put on loose silky red pants, bare-torso, and was sitting in the sedan chair, his face turned down. Then his arms began to move, as if pulled by invisible strings, and he let out a terrible scream that silenced all residual noises from us, who were watching him with a curious intensity. He shook his head violently from side to side, and a voice, deep and alien and angry, fell out of his mouth. It was not a voice I recognized, but I noticed the wide-eyed surprise and subsequent relief evident in my grandfather's and uncles' faces. They were fully aware who was speaking to them through this medium-man, a voice they knew, way before my time.

My grandfather started asking questions of the medium, and before we could hear his replies, my mother and aunties came up from behind and swatted us away. As we ran off, our laughter charting down the dark corridor, we imagined a new exciting world where the dead are never actually dead, and the living are always reaching out to them.

# With Nebuchadrezzar in Jerusalem

*William Doreski*

Just because Jeremiah complained,
God turned over Jerusalem
to Nebuchadrezzar, who burned it.

Not that we didn't enjoy
splashing fuel around the temple
and cooking the so-called great Men

in their houses; not that we minded
toppling bronze pillars and stealing
oil lamps, pots, shovels, snuffers,

copper vessels, firepans, and scraps
of gold and silver; not that we paused
an instant before we murdered

threescore men at Riblah
and set that corrupt old slob
Gedaliah in the governor's seat.

But Jeremiah bothered us
with his offhand eloquence,
his pipeline to heaven. Who explained

how to read the dry sticks and bones
in the desert? Who bribed him
to squeal on his own people?

Who directed him to pray
to the pantheon's weakest figure,
a god who'd quickly see

the logic of the anti-Semite?
Who knew he'd like the taste of ash
on his tongue, the screams in his ears?

Who taught him how to invoke
Nebuchadrezzar without smiling
like a child who just killed a fly?

# Excerpts from Seven Anglian Spells

*Andrew McCallum*

aairvhous

the house appointed for judgement
marked by an arrow bearing certain signs
to assemble the multitude

a decisive place
where we lieutenants add our arrows to
that of the headsman
pushing them into the soft belly of the earth
to signal our kinship
planting a henge that shall
over time
grow into chapels and parliaments

the house appointed for judgement
two or three men clad in the pelts of beasts
heads close
conferring on a skyline


aaron's beard

a charm against enchantment
a cure for bad milk
a sprig placed in the milk pail
before milking afresh

a sprig hid with cunning
from the priests
about one's person
against their malignancy

adderstane

earth baked hard
almost glass

a bead
a lentil
an unnatural device
disguised by name and
allegory

to protect against
the uncanniness of nature


afterwald

land taken in from the forest
stolen
domesticated

like the dogs that scavenge our touns
accepting sometimes
a kind hand
a docile word

that warn the approach of our enemies
yet slink back to the wilderness
when the spirit takes them

# Silent Messengers: Writing on Stone III

*Marja-Leena Rathje*

archival inkjet and collagraph on paper
76.2 x 50.6 cm. (20  x 30 )

Ancient writings on stone may be silent but still send powerful messages spanning great
passages of time.

# Personnage

*Holly Anderson*

*14 August 1971 (Picasso is painting)*

I lay the yolk-y yellow ground    down
now here goes my triangulated body
here is my flesh-colored jock strap
my flesh-colored wings ready for take-off.
It's hot as blisters and look how the sweat
still runs off me like a young man.
My balls hang heavy and damp.
My dark-veined stones.
Still here. Still have it. It's all in here.
I'm bringing it out bringing it forth.
I can do this. I can always do this.
The paint still listens.
I talk to the colors and they come —
from the fields this yellow mustard
from fields seen from a train trundling south
then blue canvas awning stripes
sandy Torremolinos days with mother
green seedlings black taxis in the Paris rain.    Drunk
and taking Fernande home to finally touch her    secrets.
Finger her notch her crook tongue her cleft
heft her high and bury my    self.
Now I have wings.
Flesh now yes it's always been flesh to flesh
and light shifting shapes changing course
of course I've followed the light all my life
and strung the string of shapes that tell the stories.
All the stories I've lived them all.
89 and the line still excites still makes me hard
the kernel of sex was and is and will always be there
as it should be as it must be forever and ever
so help me god.
So help me work these hands wash in pigment
wash in rapture.
The seed is there
the bursting is still there.
The bursting remains.

# Abracadabra

*Joseph Harker*

Our father used to chop off his own fingers,
pull quarters from our ears or clap his hands
to conjure Jolly Ranchers out of thin air.

We were heirs to the secret knowledge: that our father
was better than the other dads, with a gleam in his eye
that suggested he knew Important Things.
We shrilled with joy when he'd lift us onto his shoulders,
or do handstands and circle the yard.
Our birthday parties were always the best in town.
Abracadabra! and we were instant celebrities,
leading charmed elementary school lives.
Girls wore their admiration on their sleeves.

Not that we didn't have it rough.
Times are always hard for dishonest men, no matter
how many rabbits they could pull out of a hat.
Some nights we heard our father swearing;
he muttered in his sleep.

Later the novelty would wear off, and perhaps
we had our shame on our faces once too often.
None of the card tricks or magic words
held the mystery and fascination they once did.
Abracadabras won't put food on the table.
They won't keep your kids out of fights or
your hands out of the liquor cabinet. They won't dry up
sudden squalls of tears.

Maybe we should've seen it coming.
He lost the sparkle in his eyes, and fumbled the coins.
His breath was sweet with brandy. His armor rusted.
There were signs, but we thought he'd say, and now,
with a flick of the wrist, abracadabra! you can watch
me
dis
ap
pear!

It's never that simple, and it's always messy,
if you don't know how to do it right.

There's a gravestone, even though we never found a body.
The current was stronger than his soul. What if
we'd had a father that wasn't larger than life, a farmer,
a pharmacist, someone boring who wouldn't leave
his goddamn kids this way;
but then, we might accept this, move on easy.
His love was no legerdemain, so it must be this,
this passing away, this attempted suicide,
this sleight of body,
this Greatest Trick.
We wait for him at night. We whisper,
*abracadabra!*

we squeeze our eyelids tight,
count one-mis-sis-sip-pi,
open them,
and —

# No Place Like Home: Kansas 1965

*Pamela Johnson Parker*

Her bicycle and broom, her fingers bony
As catfish barbels, skin the shade of scales
Scattered from the luna's wing—oh, the witch entire

Is what I craved—her pointed hat, her widow's
Weeds trailing behind her like a burning
Bride's veil, and her voice—pure power—

*And your little dog, too.* I mimicked
That rasp for days, and I was never
Afraid… Never. What scared me were the trees,

Apple-laden branches that groped and grabbed,
False faces, wrinkling grey bark… Trees like him,
Mr. Monday, who lived across the street,

Who clutched at my hair and my red car coat.
When I wouldn't go back to the porch slanting
Before his pointy house. *Da duh, da duh*

*Da duh*—each lurching pair of steps was perfect
Iamb, a meter I'll scan again, again.
No one heard me shriek, my voice was too faint

To carry. Later, I didn't have words
To say what I cannot say. As I watched
*The Wizard of Oz* the weekend after,

Hexing, oh, I called down my worst on him,
Curses like *poppies, poppies* that sent
Dorothy and the Cowardly Lion

To sleep, to sleep. *No one will wake him up;*
*Mr. Monday lives alone, not even*
*A dog…* Before the mirror, as I murmured,

I gazed at my unfamiliar face:
*Oh, these things must be done delicately.*
*If they have ears to hear, then let them hear.*

---

# Cruickshank's Farewell

*Irene Brown*

The rumble of the Lord's Prayer
mumbled through the chapel
and, with Presbyterian necks re-set,
the piper's notes tapsilteeried their way
over the damp, sober shoulders of the mourners
who silently tutted and smirked
at the vital 'HEUCH'
that rose from the back.

# Angra Mainyu

*Harvey E. Parker*

# The Curses

*Monica Raymond*

The curses were
pleated, language folded like dense
integuments of muscle, like the heart
tougher

to bite through than
any organ. "I like it because
it is bitter," like a miner, turnip
pressed down

flesh insisting
lively through silt, no one would take that
shape, dwarf's bulb bullet, unless resisting
being

nothing, growing
downward what's possible, travel through
filth, earth, call it what you will, had your fill
knowing

dull gravity,
brown and ochre, cursing the mother
for always having to carve into her
to be.

Above ground,
easy leaves find themselves differently,
all furl and crinkle, like fans, flirtation's
light sound—

banter, repair.
These dare health, but the accordion
expansion of the root, the curses, what do
they dare?

# Voice from the Porch

*Catherine Ednie*

Open your mouth! I implore you. Don't just sit there with your face melting, tragic over trash and the cold wind.

Make a shape. Any shape. A sound. You'll feel better. More possible. More like tomorrow than today.

Wake up, honorary roadkill! There's still time. Name your comforts: dark rooms, standing up, Wanda, oranges and almonds.

Sweet, sweeet, sweet, sweet, sweeet, sweet the distance. Remember, the distance is sweet. Memories are dusty, but plush, lush, but cold. Cold and sweet as ice.

Wrapped in ice, I am telling you this. This is me, the one from the porch.

# How Time Does Things With Words

*James Toupin*

Time speaks in tongues.
In echoing castles they built
to subdue themselves, the Saxons heard
the conqueror's "ask," rightly,
as "demand." So many griefs
the language wants to tell…

Lost in the words.
Our burning, lightless, encroaches.
Now that we menace them
more than they do us,
jungles recede to forests
making and made by their rain.

Senses drain through a sieve.
"Alternative" each day
loses ground, its ending
so fallen you can no longer
tell a choice of options
from every other one.

The true name never spoken,
the book shifts back and forth —
"Jehovah" or "Elohim,"
"El Shaddai" or "Adonai,"
our Father, our King —
until the Eternal is silence.

# On Signing Your Power of Attorney

*Nancy Lazar*

In the event you lose the page you bookmarked
I shall learn how you like the bed made

In the event your head fills with down
I shall feed the ducks on the pond

In the event you find a new hobby folding origami
I shall crane my neck like a swan

In the event you grow wings
I shall expect one ride over Mount Macungie

In the event you remember there is no Mount Macungie
I shall not hold you to the above agreement

In the event you need nothing from me
I shall unlock the gates to the steeple

# Road Sign

*Steve Wing*

# Swear

*O Thiam Chin*

I was twelve years old, in Primary Six, when I saw the protests in Tiananmen Square on TV during the evening news.

Among the montage of surging crowds and marching rows of green-uniformed soldiers was an image that stuck in my head: a man, burnt to a hardened charcoal-black, tied to a smoldering bus, his wrists bound with wire, white plumes of smoke rising out of his body. His mouth was wide open, in a rigid state of screaming, his face lifted skyward and his eyes reduced to dark empty pits. Around him, a few people gawked and stared, but nobody thought of untying him from the bus.

I couldn't understand what was going on, or what had caused this violence. I tried asking my parents, but they refused to tell me anything, except to switch off the TV and to finish up my homework.

The next morning, on my way to school, heavy with the images that I had seen on TV, I chanced upon a new scribbling on the wall beside the lift: FUCK. It was a new word I hadn't seen before and I was curious to know what it meant. So I memorized it, tucking the new word into my head, and brought it to school.

During recess, I asked my good friend, Shi Hao, about the word. He laughed his head off when he heard how I tried to pronounce it.

'No, you got it wrong. It should sound like duck, like F…uck,' he admonished. I tried a few more times, but still, it came out wrong.

'What does it mean?' I asked, puzzled.

'You mean you don't know? It's a dirty word la,' he said, and before I could say anything else, our form teacher was standing beside us. With a daunting look in his eyes, Shi Hao dared me to say the word aloud. I uttered the word; my teacher heard it, twisted my ear into a knot, demanding where I had learnt such a word. Then she made me stand in front of the class the whole period, arms crossed, pulling my own ears.

As I stood there, shame-faced and scorching with a righteous rage, the image of the charred man at the Tiananmen Square, tied to the burnt bus, came to mind, and I wondered how he had gotten there, whether it was because of something he had said or done.

Maybe I thought, he had done something terribly bad to be punished in such a way; maybe, like me, he had learnt something new that he didn't fully understand, and was compelled to use it, by force or circumstance, in order to test its meaning, to know the kind of effect it would have on him, or others.

It was only many years later that I got to know the answer that turned out to be closer to the truth I already knew in my heart when I was much younger.

# Three

*Stuart Barnes*

*Beware of the rule of 3*
*What you give will get back at you*
*This lesson you must learn*
*You only get what you deserve*
—The Rule of Three

(I)
That pernicious only child of the God of Plagues and Chaos glued with Araldite a raptor-gleam
In my priest's whisky-eye, moulded into a masturbator his cold, wet fish of a fist,
Whispered slyly in my left ear, "Little boy, run like blazes! While you can, vamos, get the hell

Out of here!" then disappeared. Like a Red-backed bitch on heat on her hands and knees, I prayed
To Mr. Pilate, who whispered insidiously in my right ear, "Where's the little bastard? —
For I must burn his Birkenstocks and shear those ratty dreadlocks from his head."

I led him to the olive-moated mountain, where I kissed that son of the God of Plagues and Chaos on his grimy cheek.

\*

The Marys wept like cut grass as the sacred nails pierced the child's wrists and a sword slid in his side.
"Serves you right," I muttered, "for your father bore not only good, but its opposite, its other."

(II)
Ghastly daffodils, apples strung up in her courtyard, purple crocus shoving through frost and glass;
In a stucco council flat with a crib of pink-eyed rats and nine metres of Burmese snakes
—
Splotches like burnt-orange zeppelins, squirmed to "Whitey" and "Old Nick" — lived Mary, mad

And quite contrary. Bat-winged, bloody-eyed as her two sisters, crouched on a corner
Of the marbled kitchen table with black needles and bales she knitted: an eggshell-blue
Cloak, a sky of motes, an executioner's hood. The air was fouled by her breath, the light a sickly yellow.

Spryly that headswoman swooped to the herringbone floor, molded beneath her cauldron
Of herbs a pyramid of hieroglyphics, dry grass and sticks, fanned the language and tinder
With her terrible white bellows, and muttered dementedly, "Rise, rise, my dead fellow."

(III)
Man in black, man in black, like Ted Hughes or Johnny Cash, man in a silly Jewish hat,
No wifely striptease for that man in black, only the everyday soul-impaling, the hailing
and flaying,
Nailing wooden curlicues, Alpha and Omega, and ampersands. With hair like grey rats

And a staff of flowers, he hobbled and wobbled and cobbled and toiled for hours
For his Gothic queen bee. Eyes could no longer see, feet were swollen as plums,
Hands were like two balloons. He thought, No wonder I despise the Jews.

*

"In-sig-nif-i-cant," oozed Her Majesty to the man in black, "a flea, an Australian Ab-
origine.
You crawl lower than a dog, you can't compete with this God." The man in black's grief
grew around him
Like the Sea of Galilee. He made a wish, whispered sadly, "This earth's better off without
me."

*The title quote is taken from the introduction to "Silence" from the Portishead album Third. The other
quote — "Hands were like two balloons" — is taken from Pink Floyd's "Comfortably Numb", from The
Wall LP. (Qarrtsiluni asserts that this creative reuse is permitted under the Fair Use provision of U.S.
copyright law, which is applicable because our hosting provider, Automattic Inc., is based in the U.S.)*

# Raise the Lord: To Witnesses in My Driveway Praying on my Rebirth

*Susanna Rich*

> *Rock Me Sexy Jesus.*
> —Pam Brady and Andrew Fleming

Not to be rude, dear pious things, but why
are you praying for me like some knitting
circle — needles tap-tapping like blind
pen points trying to write on each other.
Have you no inkling?

*In His name,* you say, *you can only be
saved in His Holy Name.* But *my*
Jesus wants no fabrication, no nominal
yarn gathering or balling. I am who
He wants me to be. I strap His hands

to my headboard, bind His feet —
My Man of Proportions — My All —
My Maker of Love rising up, rising
into me. We make scenes together. My
feet poised over His feet — stigma to stigma.

I raise my arms into a cross. I am His whip.
*More,* He begs, *More pain. Be unforgivable,
so I can be big — bigger.* His mouth
is open, aching for my vinegar tongue. *Eat me,*
He cries out. I lick. I bite. I suck the wine

trickling from His breast. He burns. He sweats
into my sheets. *Mercy,* He calls out, *Mercy...*
I roll back your religious canons, rescue
Him from your Calvaries. I am not the thief
who taunts Him to save *me*. I am the one

who mounts Him over my bed, dangling over
my life. We are each other's thief — me
from below, He from above. He erects in me
His Paradise, where I come and come to Him —
My Adam, His side bleeding where He and I

die into each other, each unknowing day. Put
down your needlings, your moist ends, your double-
hooked unravelings. I don't need your loops, your
cables, your stitches. You crotchety prayers, get it —
I have Him nailed.

## The Slovenian Grandmother To Her Daughter The Platinum-Haired Dervish Just Before A Chunk of Stove Wood Was Hurled But Missed Its Blue-Eyed Mark Widely

*Holly Anderson*


YOU EAT MY HEART
YOU DRINK MY BLOOD

# sea litany

*Catherine Ednie*

o heat threat
      en me
o wave wa
      ke me
o mud jud
      ge me
o sea shel
      ter me

# Performance

*Anne Morrison Smyth*

# Escalation (Use Only as Directed)

*Adam Ford*

We appreciate that a poster
with instructions for the use
of escalators may seem patronising
and might imply we believe you have
the acumen of a four-year-old,

but we need to completely eliminate
any chance that you could point to us
and say we did not do everything
in our power to make your experience
one hundred per cent completely safe

so despite the fact that if you need help
in order to grasp these fundamentals
then a written list of what to do
on the station wall is hardly enough
to save you from yourself,

please take it in the spirit in which it was meant
when we remind you to stand to the left
and within the yellow lines, and to hold
the handrail at all times, but never to rest
anything on it, never to run either up or down

and finally to walk off promptly and
immediately step clear, and further to this
please understand that any use
which falls outside these parameters
is counter to the spirit of the contract that

you entered voluntarily into when
you placed your foot on the top or bottom stair;
having given this advice we wash our hands —
your escalation is your responsibility, so
watch your step because we can't watch it for you.

# Charge to the Jury

*Monica Raymond*

In your cool gaze, your neutrality
try to find mercy.

As you mark
the indignation of sparrows

and water seethes her bitter testimony
brackish and abused

try to seek abnegation
for the human—

some mitigating circumstance
uncertain childhood, bitter economy,

metallurgy, glamour, greed:
beauty swollen, congealed.

Try to remember this species
that dates itself by its weapons

is born hairless and has to construct
an armor of fictions,

that gravity, though pale
and guiltless as the sky

is of necessity
the opponent.

When you are tempted by the austere
precision of salutes

expressionist blur
of explosion,

try to feel kindness for this ever-breeding
lichen breathing narration.

Keep us from war, from pestilence,
from self-destruction

remember babies, joy, sages
whatever redeems us.

Be the hand on the scale
for life, try to find mercy.

# A Tree for Ezekiel

*Marly Youmans*

First of all, know this: the tree was dead,
It had already been dead for a time,
It was going to be dead a long while.
It was a stick in labyrinths of sand.
And yet, and yet—for this Ezekiel,
This dry-bone tree was clothed in chrysolite,
So that the leaves made glitterings in sun.
The bole was swathed in strips of China silk,
The twigs were mummied in gem-colored threads,
The shriveled root began to drink from earth.
A gust came from the East: the sound of wings,
And leaves turned in the wind—blue leaves and green
Looking, and each shaped like a human eye.
A dew arose from earth and bloomed as cloud,
Though in the desert, this was very strange
To see, and also there was far tumult
As if the dunes had changed to waterfalls.
The priest Ezekiel discerned a form
Among the staring blue and green of leaves,
Prismatic figure brightened by the light.
Ezekiel foretold: *Your incense lost,*
*Your limestone idols headless in the dust,*
*Your cities and all of your histories*
*Wiped from the memories of everyone . . .*
*The centuries forget your name, your love,*
*The sons and daughters raised from infancy*
*In years that are themselves forgotten things,*
*And all there is of comfort is this tree,*
*Mysterious and riddling-strange to you,*
*A rainbow covenant, its promises*
*Too far away in time for you to see.*

# Mal

*Dick Jones*

Strange word, 'stroke' — a gentle sleep
and then you wake up,
changed. Caressed by infirmity
on the brown hill, kissed
by disability as you climb
the long drive. The farmhouse tips
and, heart in crescendo,
you embrace the grass.

Indifferent sheep manoeuvre,
crowding out your sky.
You lie in a lump, adrift
at the field's edge, floating
on the dead raft
of your limbs.
The sun nails light
into your one good eye.

Near dusk her scarecrow voice
scatters your crowding dreams:
she calls you from the house,
the sound of your name
curling out of the past,
a gull-cry, fierce, impatient,
tearing at the membrane
that has dimmed your world.

Root-still, potato-eyed,
you are another species now.
Your medium is clay and saturation.
Mummified, like the bog-man
trapped by time, you lie dumbfounded,
mud-bound and uncomprehending
as the sun slips down
behind the hill.

The urgent fingers
scavenging for a heartbeat,
fluttering like bird-wings
at your throat,
are busy in the dark.
You feel nothing
of their loving panic,
their distress.

All love, all optimism, pain,
all memory, desire coarsen,
thicken into vegetable silence.
A dim siren wobbles in the dark.
And then rough hands manhandle
your clod-heavy bulk.
Night swallows the spinning light
and closes in like smoke.

# Elijah and the Raven

*Clive Hicks-Jenkins*

# Index of Contributors

**C. Albert** lives in Seattle, Washington where she divides creative time between making collage and writing poetry. Publications of her works are upcoming this fall in *Shakespeare's Monkey Review*, *Tattoo Highway*, and *Pirene's Fountain*.

**Maureen Alsop** is the author of *Apparition Wren* (Main Street Rag), *The Diction of Moths* (Ghost Road Press, pending), and several chapbooks. Winner of numerous awards, her poems have been published in a variety of journals.

**Holly Anderson's** poetry and prose has been anthologized widely and her limited edition books are in library collections in major museums, including MOMA, the Metropolitan Museum of Art, and the Victoria & Albert Museum. She is also a prolific lyricist.

**Khadija Anderson** returned last year to her native Los Angeles after 18 years exile in Seattle. Khadija's poetry has been published in print and online. She is a Butoh dancer and collaborates with her eldest son in their dance company, Tanden Butoh.

**Elizabeth Angell** is a graduate student and blogger (among other things) in New York City.

**Carrie Ann Baade** was nominated for the prestigious United States Artist Fellowship in 2007. Her work is featured in *Metamorphosis 1*. Carrie is currently an Assistant Professor of Painting and Drawing at Florida State University accompanied by her singing, polydactyl cat.

**Stuart Barnes** graduated from Monash University, Australia with a Bachelor of Arts (Literature, Philosophy). His unpublished memoir, *A Cold Decade*, was shortlisted for the Olvar Wood Fellowship Award. He's editing his first book of poetry and writing his first novel.

**Maroula Blades** is an Afro-British writer living in Berlin. Verbrecher Verlag and Cornelsen Verlag have published her short stories. An award-winning poet, she read at the Berlin Poetry Festival in 2008.

**Bryan Borland** is a poet from Little Rock, Arkansas. His cat likes to claw his expensive leather journal. He thinks the claw marks give it character.

**Patricia Bralley** lives in Atlanta and blogs at Seeing For My Self.

**Dustin Brookshire** is a poet and activist. He's the founder of *Project Verse*, *Quarrel*, and *Poetry Swap*.

**Irene Brown** lives in Scotland's capital and has been published by Calderwood Press. She provided definitions of two of the Scots words in her poem that might be unfamiliar: tapsilteerie means "topsy turvy; state of disorder," and heuch is an expression of exhilaration uttered especially while dancing.

**James Brush** is a writer and teacher living in Austin, Texas with his wife, cat, and two greyhounds. He teaches English in a juvenile correctional facility, and was once a James Michener Fellow at the Texas Center for Writers. He published his first novel, *A Place Without a Postcard*, in 2003.

**Sarah Burke** is a poet and preschool teacher living in Vermont, where the milkman delivers Ben & Jerry's to her doorstep every Monday. This is her first publication.

**Robin Chapman** studied the acquisition of speech acts by children for forty years, and now writes poetry. *Abundance*, winner of the Cider Press Review Editors' Award, is her newest book.

**O Thiam Chin's** short stories have appeared in several literary journals and anthologies. His debut collection of short stories, *Free-Falling Man*, was published in 2006 and his new collection of stories, *Never Been Better*, was released last month.

**Alex Cigale's** poems have recently appeared in the *Cafe*, *Colorado*, and *McSweeney's*. His translations from the Russian can be found in *Crossing Centuries: the New Generation in Russian Poetry*. He was born in Chernovtsy, Ukraine and lives in New York City.

**Ron Czerwien** is the owner of Avol's, a used and out-of-print bookstore in Madison, Wisconsin. His poems have appeared online in *Moria*, *Shampoo*, *nth position*, and other journals.

**William Doreski** teaches at Keene State College in New Hampshire. His most recent collection of poetry is *Waiting for the Angel* (2009). He has published three critical studies, and his essays, poetry, and reviews have appeared in many journals.

**Peg Duthie** shares a house in Nashville, Tennessee, with a small piano, a large dog, and a drawerful of knives.

**Catherine Ednie** works as a systems analyst in the New York metropolitan area. Her work appears in *In Pieces: An Anthology of Fragmentary Literature* (Impassio Press), and in various locations online.

**Karyn Eisler** is a Vancouver-based writer, educator, and interdisciplinary artist. She holds a PhD in sociology from UBC and teaches at Langara College. In a past life she worked as a radio and television broadcaster.

**Susan Elbe** is the author of *Eden in the Rearview Mirror* and a chapbook, *Light Made from Nothing*. Her poems appear or are forthcoming in many journals, including *Blackbird*, *diode*, and *Salt Hill*.

**Allen C. Fischer**, former director of marketing for a nationwide corporation, brings to poetry a background in business. His poems have appeared in *Atlanta Review*, *Prairie Schooner*, *River Styx*, and *Rattle*.

**Adam Ford** is an Australian poet with three poetry collections to his name, the latest of which is called *The Third Fruit is a Bird*.

**Caitlin Gildrien** is a writer, farmer, and sometime donut-walla in Middlebury, Vermont.

**Karen Greenbaum-Maya** is a clinical psychologist in private practice in Claremont, California. In another life, she majored in German Lit., where she read poetry for college credit. She was nominated for a 2010 Pushcart.

**Joseph Harker** is the pseudonym of a foolish twentysomething, lately located on the East Coast of the US. He dreams more than he ought to, scribbles less than he wants to, and is a textbook Libra in just about every way.

**Juleigh Howard Hobson** is a formalist poet, essayist, and short fiction writer. She has had poems nominated for both the Pushcart and the Best of the Net Award. RavensHalla Arts will be publishing her forthcoming chapbook, *The Cycle of Nine*, later this year.

**Nathan Horowitz** has three bright blue noses, six bright yellow tongues, 45 small, perfectly-shaped jet black ears, 95 hands, most of which are sleeping, and a long, long, long yellow and black stripy tail that wraps twice around the earth.

**Joe Hyam** lives in Tunbridge Wells, UK. He was a journalist, but now spends more time writing poetry and growing vegetables. Every day on his blog he posts "three fine or strange things, which, day by day, give me pleasure, and which I hope will amuse and give pleasure to others."

**Dick Jones** writes, "Initially wooed by the First World War poets and then seduced by the Beats, I have been exploring the vast territories in between since the age of 15. Grand plans for the meisterwerk have been undermined constantly either by a Much Better Idea or a sort of Chekhovian inertia."

**Angela Just** thinks she can do things better than most people—no, really, ask her friends and family. Naturally, she wishes she'd had more input into her upbringing and she's still mad about it. Muriel Karr was born in Lowell, Massachusetts on Mother's Day in 1945. Her two books of poetry are *Toward Dawn* (2002) and *Shape of Pear* (1996), both published by Bellowing Ark Press.

Canadian poet, performer, and playwright **Penn Kemp** has published twenty-five books of poetry and drama, had six plays and ten CDs produced as well as Canada's first poetry CD-ROM and several award-winning videopoems.

**Lucy Kempton** is British, living in Brittany with husband and dog, and sometimes teaching English. She is currently engaged in a call-and-response-style, online collaboration with British blogger (and *qarrtsiluni* author) Joe Hyam called Questions. She co-edited *qarrtsiluni*'s *Water* issue with Katherine Durham Oldmixon.

**Christi Krug's** work has appeared in *Umbrella*, *VoiceCatcher*, and *Defenestration*. She coaches beginning writers and blogs about the writing life.

**Barbara LaMorticella** lives in the woods outside Portland, Oregon, and hosts a poetry program on KBOO radio. She's been a finalist for the Oregon Book Award and a recipient of the Stewart Holbrook award for outstanding contribution to Oregon Literary Arts.

**Dorothee Lang** edits the *BluePrintReview*, an experimental online journal, and currently is into collaborative works. Her work has recently appeared in *LITnIMAGE*, *Counterexample Poetics*, and *Wheelhouse*.

Retired from eighteen years as a wood worker in her own business, **Nancy Lazar** now concentrates on creative writing after moving to her home in the foothills of the Pocono Mountains. Her poem based on "The Waste Land" by T.S. Eliot was chosen and recorded for Soundzine.

**Amy MacLennan** has been published or has work forthcoming in *Hayden's Ferry Review*, *River Styx*, and *Rattle*. Her poems are forthcoming in the anthologies *Not a Muse* from Haven Books and *Eating Her Wedding Dress: A Collection of Clothing Poems* from Ragged Sky Press.

**Julia Martin** is a lapsed lawyer who now battles the apocalypse by bringing new books and pleasure reading to low-income children in the Chicago area.

**Maya Massar** is a poet who dances, loves Africa, and sings to celestial bodies and stones. She is also a painter who has exhibited Vancouver, B.C.'s East Side Culture Crawl.

**Andrew McCallum** is a widely published and award-winning poet from southern Scotland. The countryside around his home is littered with relics of his forebears, who speak through them as far back as mesolithic times, and with whom Andrew strongly identifies in his poetry.

**Colleen McKee** is the author of a collection of poetry, *My Hot Little Tomato* (Cherry Pie, 2007) and co-editor of an anthology of personal narratives, *Are We Feeling Better Yet? Women Speak About Health Care in America* (PenUltimate, 2008).

**Ann E. Michael** is a poet, essayist, librettist, and educator who lives in Eastern Pennsylvania. She holds an MFA in creative writing from Goddard College and is a rostered Artist-in-Education with the Pennsylvania Council on the Arts.

**M.V. Montgomery's** first collection of poems, *Strange Conveyances*, will be published by the Plain View Press. A second book, a pamphlet of historical poems titled *Joshu Holds a Press Conference*, will be published in 2010 by the Conversation Paperpress.

**David Need** lives in Durham, North Carolina, and teaches Central and South Asian Religion and Poetry at Duke University. His poetry and essays have appeared or will appear in *Talisman*, *Hambone*, and on *MiPoesias*. He is an avid blogger.

**Richard Nester** is a former fellow of the Fine Arts Work Center in Provincetown, and has published in a number of locations including *Ploughshares*, *Seneca Review*, *Sycamore Review*, and *Tikkun*.

**Oriana** leads a double—sometimes a triple—life by the sea; the cold Pacific Ocean near San Diego.

**Christina Pacosz** has been writing and publishing prose and poetry for almost half a century. She has been teaching urban youth for the past decade on both sides of the Missouri/Kansas state line where she lives with her husband.

**Harvey E. Parker** was a visual artist who teaches Gifted and Talented in four public schools. His interests included mythology, history, maps, and books. His most recent work was in ATC (Artist Trading Card) format, the only requirement being that the finished piece be 2.5 x 3.5 inches, the size of a standard playing card.

**Pamela Johnson Parker** is a medical editor and adjunct professor in creative writing and poetry. Her inaugural collection *A Walk Through the Memory Palace* was the winner of qarrtsiluni's 2009 poetry chapbook contest. Her poems, flash fiction, and essays have been widely published.

**Zoe Polach** is from the Maryland suburbs of D.C. She started as a freshman at the University of Chicago this fall.

**Marja-Leena Rathje** is a Finnish-Canadian artist specializing in printmaking and photography. She is crazy about weathered rocks, prehistoric art, and the archaeology of past, present and future. She lives and works in Vancouver.

**Francis Raven** is a graduate student in philosophy at Temple University. His books include *5-Haifun: Of Being Divisible* (Blue Lion Books, 2008), *Shifting the Question More Complicated* (Otoliths, 2007), and the novel *Inverted Curvatures* (Spuyten Duyvil, 2005).

**Monica Raymond** won the Castillo Prize in political theater for her play *The Owl Girl*, which is about two families in an unnamed Middle Eastern country who both have keys to the same house. Her poetry has been published in numerous journals and magazines.

**Jane Rice** lives in San Francisco and pursues her interests in poetry, art and art history. She is the author of a letterpress chapbook entitled *Portrait Sitters*.

**Susanna Rich** is a 2009 Emmy Award nominee for the poetry she wrote and recorded for Craig Lindvahl's documentary *Cobb Field*. She is a Fulbright Fellow in Creative Writing and Professor of English and Distinguished Teacher at Kean University in New Jersey.

**Susan Roney-O'Brien** teaches, reads for the *Worcester Review*, and writes. Her work has appeared in *Yankee*, *Prairie Schooner*, and the *Christian Science Monitor*. She has won the New England Association of Teachers of English "Poet of the Year" award.

**Marjorie Stamm Rosenfeld** has been published both nationally and internationally in journals, books, and anthologies and on the Internet. She has done poetry therapy with forensic patients at St. Elizabeth's Hospital and maintains three websites on perished Jewish communities in Eastern Europe.

**cin salach** has been performing and publishing in Chicago for over 20 years. She is both baffled by and grateful for online submissions of poetry. Actually, she is baffled and grateful by/for most things.

**Ayesha Saldanha** is a writer, translator, and blogger based in Bahrain.

**Ian Singleton** attends Emerson College in Boston as an MFA student and works as a librarian at Harvard University. He teaches in the PEN Prison Writing Program. His translation of a story by Rainer Maria Rilke was published in *Knock*.

Prize-winning photographer **Anne Morrison Smyth** grew up in Ripton, Vermont and in Cambridge, Massachusetts. Anne's love for wildernesses of all kinds informs her work with an intimate, unflinching celebration of the diverse small realities that create a larger truth.

**Paul Stevens**, formerly of Leeds and Harrogate, late of The Strand, has taken up permanent residence in the Seventeenth Century where he may be found at the Mermaid Tavern, roistering intemperately and waving a tattered copy of *The Flea* broadsheets.

**Jeneva Stone** wears many hats: poet, blogger, mother, federal employee, practical g/i nurse, interpreter of EOBs, queen of medical necessity letters, keeper of the family exchequer, unlicensed physical therapist, and knowledgeable wheelchair mechanic.

**Robin Susanto** lives in Vancouver, Canada. He takes photographs not as proof of having been, but as a way to slow down the act of seeing.

**Kaz Sussman** is a carpenter by trade, an anarchist by nature, and an expatriate New Yorker by circumstance. He got into poetry (just like everyone else) because he knows that's where the big bucks are. He now lives in a home he built in Oregon from recycled rejection letters.

**Andrew Topel**, standing at 5 feet 11 inches, could indeed be considered short. He describes his work as "solo and collaborative visualanguage and wreyeting."

**James Toupin** is a government lawyer who lives in Washington. He writes, "legal instruments are by definition words of power, [*qarrtsiluni's*] theme treads on ground my poetry seems to go over and over. However, it ventures onto that ground mostly in a religious vein, reflecting a mixed Jewish and Christian heritage."

**Linda Umans** has had work published on- and off-line, recently in *Beauty/Truth: Journal of Ekphrastic Poetry*. She is a traveler but a native of New York City where she lives and works.

**Wendy Vardaman** has a Ph.D. in English from University of Pennsylvania. She is co-editor of the Wisconsin poetry journal *Verse Wisconsin* (formerly *Free Verse*) and works for a youth theater, The Young Shakespeare Players.

**Julene Tripp Weaver** has a chapbook, *Case Walking: An AIDS Case Manager Wails Her Blues*, based on her work in HIV Services. A poem from this chapbook was featured on *The Writer's Almanac*. Her poetry has been published in many journals and anthologies.

**Bev Wigney** is a photographer, writer, artist, and naturalist who recently left her home of 31 years on a farm in eastern Ontario after the death of her husband, Don, and is now traveling around North America in a van with her two collies.

**Steve Wing** is a visual artist and writer whose work reflects his appreciation for the extraordinary in ordinary days and places. He lives in Florida, where he takes dawn photos on his way to work in an academic institution.

**Christopher Woods** lives in Houston and Chappell Hill, Texas. His online gallery is Moonbird Hill Arts.

**Marly Youmans** recently saw the publication of her seventh book, *Val/Orson*. Set among the tree sitters of California's redwoods, the story takes its inspiration from the legendary tale of Valentine and Orson and the forest romances of Shakespeare.

**Clive Hicks-Jenkins** has worked as an actor in film and on TV, and was a highly successful choreographer, director, and stage designer before switching his focus to painting in the mid-90s. In 2008 he was nominated a Royal Cambrian Academician.

www.ingramcontent.com/pod-product-compliance
Lightning Source LLC
Chambersburg PA
CBHW072003170626
46813CB00005B/1991

* 9 7 8 0 9 8 6 6 9 0 9 0 7 *